8 Steps to Being a
Great Mom
working

Tips for maintaining your sanity
while juggling work and motherhood

By Gretchen Gagel

8 Steps to Being a Great Working Mom
by Gretchen Gagel

For information, contact BDI Publishers, Atlanta, Georgia, bdipublishers@gmail.com.

ISBN: 978-0-9962646-1-7

FIRST EDITION

Please note that some of the names of women in the book have been changed for privacy reasons.

BDI Publishers
Atlanta, Georgia

PRAISE FOR
8 STEPS TO BEING A GREAT
WORKING MOM

"I was excited to contribute to 'Eight Steps,' as I have learned so much over the years as a working mother. The reality is, you can have a career and be a mother—and do well at both! Gretchen does a great job of sharing personal stories from a very diverse group of women. The tips they give are practical, meaningful and easy to adopt."

—Margaret Kelly, retired CEO, RE/MAX

"I really can't believe that Gretchen was able to write this book with all that she does. Thinking about our working relationship, I can honestly say that Gretchen probably talks about stories of her children as much as her work experiences. I know Gretchen's children are cared for and loved by her. Gretchen's ability to manage both sides of her life is nothing short of remarkable."

—Michael Mayra, construction group manager, General Motors

"Having known Gretchen for over twenty years as both a colleague and a friend, I can attest to her dedication and effectiveness as a mom and a professional. Beyond her work and kids, Gretchen has made time for a robust personal life, involvement in numerous local organizations, and two advanced degrees. While her intellect is certainly above average, she makes do with the same twenty-four hours as the rest of us. This book is a great treatise on managing the seemingly impossible."

—Hugh L Rice, senior chairman, FMI Corporation

"In the twenty years I've known Gretchen, she has made a significant contribution to the construction industry while still 'being there' for her kids at the important turns. I totally agree with her point that there's no such thing as balance and that working moms need to prioritize what's important and 'let go of the rest.' I'm a working mom, too, and I think that gave my daughter an appreciation of work and making a contribution. Gretchen is an accomplished writer, and many women will benefit from these fun-to-read eight steps."

—Janice L. Tuchman, editor-in-chief,
Engineering News-Record

"Gretchen worked tirelessly as assistant dean of Daniels to engage the alumni community here in Chicago, and I know from our friendship that her kids mean the world to her. All of my kids will benefit from the practical advice in this book, and the humor is pure Gretchen."

—Tom Buddig, partner, Carl Buddig and Company

"I'm so thrilled that Gretchen's guest-lecturing in my business courses prompted her to go back for her PhD. She is a marvel student, teacher, leader and a great mom— you can tell by the way she talks about her children. I was a working mom and can relate to this book!"

—Karen Newman, professor emerita and former dean,
Daniels College of Business, University of Denver

"In her two years as assistant dean of the Daniels College of Business, Gretchen met hundreds of alumni across the country and made those of us in New York feel a much stronger connection to the school. And I never saw Gretchen when she wasn't talking about her kids—their hockey, college searches, etc. This book is an outstanding reflection of her dedication to her work and her kids and will be of great value to great working moms everywhere."

—Michael Belsky, University of Denver, class of 1976

"I've worked with Gretchen to develop successful project teams since she was pregnant with Holden during my leadership of the Baltimore Ravens Stadium Project in 1995—where she had the good sense not to do the trust fall at Outward Bound! Gretchen's passion for both her work and her kids is evident in everything she does. She is certainly among the most talented and hard-working people I've ever worked with, and this book is a gift to working moms everywhere to help explain her secrets."

—Alice Hoffman, PE, president, Hoffman
Management Partners, LLC

"Not only is this book great for working moms, but we dads can learn plenty. I wish I had read this on the front end of my parental journey. Throughout our twenty-year friendship, I have admired Gretchen for her dedication to her family and work and her passion for a full life. This is a quick must-read with something for every parent."

—Ben Brahinsky, founder, Leap Financial

"Gretchen brings a thoughtful, humorous and common-sense approach to dealing with the busyness and craziness that all mothers face in their lives. She provides great advice for moms as well as all men and women juggling the multiple roles we each play."

—Jill S. Tietjen, PE, CEO,
National Women's Hall of Fame.

"I moved in across the street from Gretchen a year before her children were born, when we were both traveling every week, and am 'Aunt Carol' to her kids. She has done a masterful job of making career decisions that fulfilled her needs and ensured that she was there for her children. Holden and Regan have become outstanding young adults. I know Gretchen wrote this book with the heartfelt intention of helping working moms realize that they can have fulfilling careers and be great moms."

—Carol Burt, Healthcare Executive, Board Member
and Operating Partner

"As peer foundation presidents, I know Gretchen's work to improve our Denver community. As friends, I know her love for her children. Gretchen's tips for working moms are practical, and I know she speaks from the heart."

—Linda Childears, president & CEO, The Daniels Fund

"Working closely with Gretchen at the Women's Foundation of Colorado gave me a great opportunity to see firsthand how hard Gretchen worked to juggle her work and family lives. Holden and Regan were regularly involved in her work and clearly the focus of her attention, even while working long hours on our campaign. I plan to share this book!"

—Mary Sissel, former board chair,
The Women's Foundation of Colorado

"Gretchen is a tremendous role model and epitomizes what it means to be a woman who is fiercely dedicated to her family and deeply rewarded by her work. I know that women around the world will benefit from her story, and I am grateful to her for giving so much of herself through this book and sharing intimate stories of her challenges as a working mom."

—Avery Bang, CEO, Bridges to Prosperity

"I have worked for Gretchen on and off for fourteen years. Being a part of her family and caring for her children was an amazing experience for me. The organization skills, communication and support team that Gretchen speaks of really are the key to a successful way of working and managing a family, a household and child care."

—Adele Groditski, caregiver and personal assistant

"My work as a pediatrician exposes me to the significant challenges working moms face in juggling their careers and family. Gretchen speaks from the heart in sharing these intimate feelings of guilt and angst she and others have experienced. I'm certain this book will make a difference in the lives of those who read it."

—Dean Prina, pediatrician

"Gretchen may say in her book that there is no such thing as balance, but she certainly has many robust areas of life. We can now add accomplished author! In her book, she generously shares her stories about the challenges of working while raising children and adds suggestions from her struggles to overcome the obstacles. If you are a working mom, you will recognize yourself in her experiences and will be inspired to try a tip or two. After all, you're already a great mom, just like Gretchen!"

—Barbara Bridges, Women+Film Founder

"When you first asked me to be a part of your book, I had been laid off from my job for the second time not much earlier. My family and I were moving out of state and I knew I would be getting back to work soon. I quickly went back to work, and what helped in more ways than I expected was looking back and remembering everyone else's tips, including what I was saying to others."

—Rachel Contizano

CONTENTS

DEDICATION

This book is dedicated to my mom, Jane Gagel, who passed away in 2013. She was, and will always be, my biggest fan, and I love her dearly. And it is dedicated to my wonderful kids, Holden and Regan, who gave me the greatest gift of my life, motherhood. It is also dedicated to my ex-husband, Dan McComb, who is a caring father and partner in raising our kids, and to my sister Pam Gagel and friend Annie Hoskinson, who are as much moms to my kids as I am. Finally, it is dedicated to my amazing partner in life, Philip. You are a good man and I love you.

ACKNOWLEDGMENTS

My thanks to everyone who contributed to the book – you are all amazing and I'm grateful to each and every one of you. My thanks also to the women of Warren Village who contributed invaluable insight.

I am grateful to my editor, Toni Robino of Windword Literary Services, who encouraged me to finish this book. Your guidance has been outstanding and I appreciate your wisdom and support.

Most important, I am thankful to my kids, Holden and Regan. You are both a joy and have taught me so much about unconditional love. Who knew that being a mom would be the greatest experience of my life?! I love you both.

FOREWARD

In 1982 I was a newly single mom of two wonderful children, ages ten and six, and the CEO of a newly founded industrial construction company. Oh how I wish I had had Gretchen Gagel's book, *The 8 Steps to Being a Great Working Mom*, to help me through that next decade. I might not have needed a therapist!

Gretchen's book took me right back to those moments of great guilt, high stress, total exhaustion, and amazing joy. But now there's a survival guide for working moms. Actually, her book is a guide for thriving while mothering and working and for learning to enjoy the journey.

Her book starts with "Getting Over Guilt." Of course! And it ends with "You Are Worth It," about the importance of taking care of yourself. Every chapter is direct, funny, sensitive, insightful, and, most of all, helpful. And each chapter is right on target with a summary and exercises at the end to help you better understand yourself and find solutions and real compassion in your heart for you. But the best part is, Gretchen supplies us with very real and concrete suggestions for how to manage, balance, and celebrate our lives and the multiple roles we play in them.

The 8 Steps to Being a Great Working Mom is a gift for every working mom and a beautiful reflection of the common sense, dedication, and loving spirit of Gretchen Gagel. Enjoy. It will make your life easier.

Barb Grogan

INTRODUCTION

Why did I write this book? And who am I to be giving you advice?

I'm a mom who works outside the home. My son and daughter were born in 1996 and '97, thirteen months apart, and after their births I found myself thrust into the three-ring-circus of working motherhood without any preparation. At the time, I was a management consultant who traveled four days a week, forty-six weeks a year. Since then, I've had four jobs, all demanding and most requiring travel.

While raising my kids, I struggled to maintain my sanity and figure out how to be a great working mom. I wrote the first draft of this book twelve years ago when my kids were still young and I was happily married to my husband, Dan. I decided to finish it four years after our divorce. I thought when I revisited what I'd written so many years ago, I'd have different advice or insights, but that wasn't the case. What I did have was twelve more years of experience and stories to share. But the basic steps that keep me sane and help me be a great working mom remain the same.

Author Steven Covey says women are "givers" in life. We give to our partners, our family and our kids, but what do we give to ourselves? Having a job outside the home may be something we "give" ourselves to be fulfilled, or it may be a financial necessity. Either way, working moms at times feel like we're on the edge of insanity, like we're struggling to be great moms and successful businesswomen, too. Thus, this book. If one woman reads one thing in this book that makes her life easier, it will have been worth every minute I've squeezed out of my hectic life to write it.

What you will find in this book are common-sense approaches to making your life easier. What you will not find are silver bullets. I am not a psychologist, life strategist or magician. I'm a mom who struggles every day to juggle the demands of a career and a family. No mom is perfect and no one has all the answers, but there are techniques to mitigate the stress we all face. Each chapter ends with a series of exercises that will help you think through your own personal steps toward juggling work and motherhood. I know you're a great mom, and these questions and your answers will help to increase the confidence you have in yourself.

It also helps to understand that we're all in the same boat and face similar challenges, so I've included insights and tips from many of my friends and colleagues in this book. I also held a focus group for residents of Warren Village, a transitional housing program for single moms in Denver that will receive a portion of the proceeds from this book. I wanted to make sure the book reflected the ideas of women with different types of jobs and different levels of resources.

I've tried to write in a concise format because I know you barely have enough time to read food labels, let alone books. The book is organized so that you can read it from start to finish or skip around, starting with the chapters that matter most to you.

I sincerely hope the ideas and tips in this book will help you feel less stress, maintain your sanity and have more fun and fulfillment with your kids and with your work.

To read and share more stories, and see what's working for other great working moms, visit our website, www. greatworkingmoms.com, join our LinkedIn Group, Great Working Moms; like us on Facebook at Great Working Moms, and follow us on twitter @greatworkingmom. You can also reach me at gretchen@greatworkingmoms.com.

STEP ONE

It's OK to Work
Getting Over the Guilt

I'd been looking forward to my son's seventh-grade band concert all day. Holden played the baritone and I couldn't have been more proud of him. I had an evening meeting, my last meeting as a member of the Board of Directors of Denver's Anchor Center for Blind Children. I made sure Alice Applebaum, the executive director, knew I needed to leave the meeting by six-thirty because of the concert.

Everything was going like clockwork until I stood up to leave. It turned out that since it was my last meeting, the other board members had a gift for me. It was all I could do to stop myself from looking at my watch as these sincerely grateful people shared kind words of appreciation for the job I'd done. When the last person finished, I sprinted to my car and took off for my son's school. The concert was scheduled to start at seven and it was nearly seven fifteen.

I managed to hit every red light and heavy traffic, and by the time I ran in the front door of the school, it was seven forty-five. I raced down the hall, wishing I were wearing running shoes instead of high heels, and as I neared the gymnasium, I could hear someone playing the baritone. Not just someone, actually—I could tell it was Holden.

And he was playing a solo.

I ran faster, slid around the corner and barreled through the doors of the gym. The bleachers, filled with hundreds of parents watching the concert, were right across from the door, so I couldn't just rush in. Instead, I discreetly sneaked around the corner so I could see Holden and hear the last thirty seconds of the solo. It was beautiful.

After the concert, I asked Holden, "Why didn't you tell me you had a solo?" He said, "I was doing it as a surprise for Mother's Day."

My heart sank. Despite the plan I'd had in place to get there on time, I nearly missed my son's Mother's Day surprise. Even though he assured me that it was OK that I'd been late, it broke my heart to imagine him looking for me in the bleachers and not finding me there. I was grateful that I hadn't missed the whole thing, but I went to bed that night with a serious case of guilt, and I'm betting that every working mom reading this book can relate to that feeling. Only recently did I learn that not only did Holden understand but that he was a little relieved because doing the solo had put a lot of pressure on him. "I didn't want you to see me mess up," he said. I was totally surprised to hear this.

The first and most important step to being a great working mom is to find ways to deal with the inevitable guilt of not always being everywhere we wish we could be with our kids. We need to have confidence that we're great moms and feel good about ourselves. To do this, we have to feel good about our decision to work outside the home as we're raising our kids. Whether we're passionate about our work, simply enjoy working or have no other choice financially, the more we embrace our role as working moms, the more effective we can be at home and at work.

Working outside the home does not negatively affect our kids. In fact, I believe it's had a positive impact on my kids, and now that they're young adults, they agree. You'll hear more from my kids later.

Feeling guilty rarely produces helpful results. It drains our vital energy and robs us of the joy our kids offer us every single day. It also diminishes our ability to be our very best when we're at work. It's not possible for real women to be perfect moms or perfect employees. The idea of being both is a crazy standard that we need to let go of. Whether you want to work or you have to work, I'm hoping that the ideas and strategies in this book make your life a little easier and a lot saner. If we feel guilt as working moms, let's face it instead of pretending we're handling everything perfectly.

Quelling the 'Internal Guilt'

"Internal guilt," the guilt we inflict on ourselves, can be our own worst enemy. Most working moms experience some level of guilt: "I'm a bad mom because I don't want to stay home with my kids"; "I'm a bad mom because I can't afford to stay home with my kids"; "I should be the one caring for them. No one can care for my kids as well as I can." I've wrestled with these kinds of thoughts, and I can almost guarantee that you have, too. The majority of women I surveyed for this book answered "yes" to the question "Did you ever feel guilty working and not being a stay-at-home mom?"

For many women, guilt rears its ugly head as we make the transition from maternity leave back into the outside working world. I decided to go back to work when Holden, my first child, was six weeks old. I felt ready and I wanted to take more time off later when he was older. Two of my friends who had had their first babies around the same time I had Holden decided to take three months off, and they both had a hard time returning to work. Hearing them lament having to leave their babies opened the floodgates of self-induced guilt for me. *Why do I want to go back? Don't I want to be with my child? Is there something wrong with me?* Comparing our choices with those of other women isn't a fair comparison because we're individuals, but that doesn't stop us from doing it. I love my kids dearly, but I also love my job and it puts food on the table and a roof over our heads.

Getting Over the Internal Guilt

It took me quite some time to get over these self-induced feelings of guilt, and I probably still have some lurking in my mind, but I discovered some techniques to help quell the "internal guilt" voice that I hope will work for you:

- Remind yourself that working provides for your family.

- Keep a journal and reflect on all the positive things about working outside the home. Here's my list:

  o It gave my husband, mom and sister the opportunity to have a more meaningful relationship with my kids.

  o Because of the caregivers and child-care providers, my kids learned to relate to people who were different from our family members.

  o My kids understand my work and my passion for it, and working was part of being a good role model for them.

- o I got a much-needed and deserved break from my kids!

- o I am energized by my clients and the work that I do, and I brought that energy to my family life.

- o My kids felt loved by many people and were comfortable and secure knowing that so many people, including their caregivers, loved them.

  We lived a comfortable life financially.

- Identify what you like most about the work you do and how it helps others or contributes to society. Feeling good about what you do will help you to feel happier, and that will benefit your family. I loved my work and it made me a better mom because I was happy and fulfilled. Our happiness spills over into our relationships with our kids.

- If you choose to work outside the home, make a list of reasons that you wouldn't make a great stay-at-home mom and reasons that you do make a *great mom*. I knew in my heart that I would have made a terrible stay-at-home mom. I really didn't have the patience for it. One Christmas when the kids were two and three and our caregiver took two weeks off, I lost eight pounds and was exhausted when she returned. I'm certain the kids were ready to have her back!

People often focus on what they see as the downside of my job, which is the travel. But there are many upsides to this "downside." My travel actually affords me the chance to spend time with my kids. I was able to have dinner with my son in Rolla, Missouri, in the fall of his freshman year because I was close by in St. Louis on business. I was able to attend many of my daughter's out-of-state hockey tournaments because of my ability to tie them in to business trips. My kids have been to Hawaii, France, Italy, Germany and Switzerland via the miles I've earned traveling. My son and daughter are both well-adjusted and independent, and I have the satisfaction of knowing that my career contributed to this.

But even with this knowledge, there are some memories that haunt me. In 2010 when I was commuting from Denver to San Francisco every other week, the kids lived with their dad when I wasn't in Denver. One day our caregiver called me and said Regan was extremely upset. When she put Regan on the phone, she told me through her sobs that one of the boys in her eighth-grade French class had committed suicide.

I felt so sad that I couldn't be there to wrap my arms around my daughter. I consoled her as best I could over the phone, coached the caregiver a bit on what to do, and called Regan's dad and my sister so that they could both be there for her. I felt horrible, but other people stepped in, and I was grateful for that.

I'd be lying if I said I didn't wish I could have been there that day and, for that matter, every day to hear how my kids' days had been and help them with their homework. No decision is perfect—there are things I missed being a working mom—but for me, the positives outweigh the negatives, and they can for you, too. I hope that hearing the insights and stories of the other working moms interviewed for this book will help you to let go of your guilt.

You *are* a great mom.

Deflecting the Guilt That Others Impose

Even more frustrating than the guilt we impose on ourselves is the insensitive guilt that others inflict on us whether they're aware they're doing so or not.

I could share a thousand of these stories, but the following one is a good representation. Since my work required significant air travel, I spent a lot of time on airplanes. People sitting next to me would often see the United "1K" luggage tag on my briefcase indicating that I flew more than a hundred thousand miles a year and would ask what I did. Nearly every week the next question was consistently, "You don't have kids, do you?" When I told them I did, the next question was *always*, "Who watches the kids while you're gone?" It wasn't the question that irked me—it was the judgmental tone in their voices that implied that I should be home watching them myself.

This attitude really struck a nerve, and at some point I started experimenting with different responses. One day I couldn't resist having a little fun with my seatmate. When he asked, "Who watches your kids while you're gone?" I smiled and said, "Oh, I just leave them in the trunk of my car with a little food and water at the airport, and so far it seems to be working out just fine." That pretty much ended the conversation!

The point is, as long as we feel good about what we're doing, why should we care about what anyone else thinks? We know we shouldn't care, but the judgments of others can still hit a nerve.

When I became pregnant with my first child, I was working as a management consultant in the construction industry, and several of my clients asked me if my husband was going to *let* me keep working after the baby came. It was as if I were working only at the whim of my husband, and there was an assumption that we could easily afford for me to stop working. I must admit that my husband, understanding the equality of our relationship, found this much more humorous than I did.

I told my boss, Lou, that clients were saying these kinds of things to me, but I'm not sure he believed me until he heard it himself. We were at a cocktail party talking to one of our clients, the owner of a general contracting firm, and at one point the gentleman turned to Lou and asked, "Have you started looking for Gretchen's replacement yet?" Lou gave me an "Is there something I should know?" look, and I shook my head. The client proceeded to say that the yearnings that God put in me to be a mom would overcome my yearnings to have a career, that I would basically come to my senses and realize what my appropriate role is in the world and quit my job. Lou's jaw hit the floor!

Sidestepping the External Guilt Trip

Some women don't feel guilty so much as they feel angry that others judge them. "I never felt guilty so much as I felt angry about the 'mommy wars,' " one of the women interviewed shared. "My choices (and I use that term loosely) belong to me alone, and no one else gets to judge." It seems that everyone has an opinion on whether moms should work, and they're not shy about sharing it, whether we care to hear it or not. People who inflict their opinions on me without any thought for my feelings continually amaze me, but they're out there. Sometimes they seem determined to say things to us that trigger our guilt, as if we don't have enough already. I've experienced the entire spectrum of guilt over the years, but I can honestly say I'm a better mom for working, and I believe my kids are better off because of that.

Many of the women interviewed said they could ignore what strangers said but had a harder time ignoring it when their own moms laid on the guilt. Margaret Kelly, retired CEO, RE/MAX understood that her mom was basing her belief that moms should stay home with their kids on her traditional values. She had stayed home and raised six kids. "My mom would call and say, 'When are you going to stay home with your babies?'" Margaret said. "And I'd say, 'Well, Mom, you know I'm CEO of RE/MAX now and my babies are in high school.'

"When I first went back to work, I doubted myself, thinking, 'Wow, maybe I am wrong.' but then, fortunately, we all gain maturity and wisdom and get enough bumps and bruises that we know that working is OK, that our kids will be fine and we'll be fine."

But the bumps still hurt. "When my oldest son, Patrick, was in elementary school, he got upset one night at dinner because there was something or other that I couldn't do with him because I was working," Margaret said. "He burst into tears and said, 'My wife is never gonna work. She's gonna be home with the kids.' I felt horrible. I was in tears that night, thinking that Patrick might really feel neglected somehow. Fast-forward to his twenties and one day he said, 'I'm looking for a woman who's my equal, who's very confident and who wants to work.' And I said, 'Whoa, whoa, whoa, wait a minute. What about you wanting somebody who's going to stay home with kids and all that?' And he said, 'What? I never said that.' And

I said, 'So, after ten years I can pull the knife back out of my heart?' He and my husband both started laughing. Now both of my sons say, 'We don't want a woman that we have to make every decision for. We want a partner, we want somebody with some leadership abilities.' It's so refreshing to hear that!

"Kids are going to say things that do guilt you, but the fact is, as long as they know they're loved and you have the time for them, they're not harmed. So what I've always told women is, choose the things that really fill your heart that you feel you need to do, and just realize you're always going to have guilt."

Many working moms agree that the guilt can be especially challenging when our kids are too young to understand why we leave every day or where we go. But as our kids get older, we can talk to them about what we do and why it makes us feel fulfilled. Or we can share why we need to work to be able to provide them with a home and clothes or to pay for the sports, music lessons or other activities they enjoy. While we don't want our kids to feel burdened with financial pressures (isn't that one of the best things about being a child?), talking to them about why we work for money as well as for satisfaction is an important primer for life. Sharing how we budget our money and make spending decisions helps our kids to understand why we can't always be where they want us to be and why we don't buy whatever they want when they want it. My parents never discussed our financial situation, so I grew up not truly understanding the economics of life.

Tips for Dealing with the Guilt

Here's a sampling of what working moms, past and present, have to say about dealing with the guilt:

"I realized if I worked and I wasn't at home, I would guilt myself. If I was home and not working, I would guilt myself ... So realize that you will have guilt no matter what and choose the right path for you."

—Margaret Kelly, retired CEO, RE/MAX

"Every weekend my ten-year-old daughter and I do something fun together, just the two of us. I save $5 to $10 each week so we can go to a bargain cinema, go out for breakfast or pack a picnic. I make it a priority to enjoy spending time together every week."

—Ruby, single working mom

"I try to take a couple days a month where I can pick up my sons in car line at school so they don't have to go to the after-school program every day. When Cole and Brody see me in the car line, their faces light up and they stand a little straighter. Just saying this makes me feel a little sad for them, and guilty."

—Jody Camp, director of family planning programs, Colorado Department of Public Health and Environment

"I know that the work I'm doing matters and that my kids are thriving, so we just keep marching forward."

—Deidre Bacala, campaign director, American Cancer Society

"I feel guilty if I can't be at home when I'm needed, especially when I travel. But I feel I'm a better mom by working."

—Betsy Mordecai, founder and president, MorEvents Inc.

"I stopped working and stayed at home full time with my girls when they were very young, but that left me unsatisfied, so I divorced, went back to work and did it all by myself, and it was actually easier."

—Jeanne Saunders, founder, Saunders Financial

"I made just about all my son's games and concerts and we did lots of great activities together, but I felt sad that I had to miss a few. I absolutely know, however, that I was a better, more balanced person as a result of my work and that when I did spend time with my son, it was with 100 percent focus. Being a working mom helped me to prioritize and to appreciate every moment of 'mom time' I had."

—Sharon Knight, president and CEO, Warren Village

"I still feel guilty sometimes, but I overcame a lot of the guilt by going to part-time and by talking to other women who were feeling the same way I was feeling. It was easier to know that there were other women who were going through the same situation."

—Lora Ledermann, creative director, Scream Agency

It's OK to Not Feel Guilty

So, there's no doubt that many working moms are still dealing with guilt, but I think it's promising that a number of the moms interviewed for this book don't feel guilty, or at least not often or not very much.

"I didn't feel guilty about working, so I felt out of step with my friends that were all worrying about it," says Susan Walters, development operations director for the Dallas Women's Foundation. "I have a lot of friends who've been traumatized by the whole mommy-priorities thing, and I just never felt like that. I think you can't second-guess yourself. You just have to do what you gotta do. Take advantage of whatever you have, whatever people you have in your life, co-workers or good baby-sitters or your spouse or whatever. Make a choice and move on. Because the more time you spend revisiting whether or not you should be working, the more miserable you'll probably feel."

Lisa Walker, business manager for Pax Christi Catholic Church in Littleton, Colorado, says, "Working was just something I had to do for myself. And I never once felt guilty about it. I don't think that as an employee, I could be as effective or productive if I felt bad about being there. I can understand the guilt feeling, but since my parents took care of our kids, I felt completely comfortable going to work.

"My mom owned an antique shop for years, and one of the things she always said was that her whole life didn't revolve around being a mom and that she had her own life, too. So I was spared the guilt that a lot of women my generation feel because their own moms didn't work."

It's encouraging to hear women who feel little to no guilt about working, and I can only hope that their numbers will steadily increase. As for those of us still working through guilt, we might as well accept it and look for ways to mitigate our feelings. One way to avoid getting stuck in this no-win guilt vortex is to turn your attention to how your kids and you are benefiting because you're working. What would the drawbacks be if you weren't working? Answering these questions can help you to maintain a more realistic view of your situation.

The Power of Being Truly Present

Both my kids have told me they really appreciate the time and attention I gave them when I was home. When Holden was interviewed for this book, he said, "I'm really grateful that she realized that she was gone a lot and that she made sure we knew that she loved us. We knew that just because she was gone didn't mean she didn't care. And when she was home, she devoted her time to us and sacrificed a lot. It was all about us; where did we want to go, what did we want to do?

"We'd hang out, she'd make dinner. She participated in our lives as much as she could. And when she had vacation time, she used all her frequent-flier miles on us. When she was away when we were younger, there were a lot of phone calls. As we got older and got our own phones, she was texting with us, just making sure that we knew that she was thinking about us and that she missed us."

Regan said, "When she was home it was all about being with Holden and me. She had all sorts of special little rituals for us, like making cookies for me after school and making chocolate chip pancakes and sausage for Holden on weekends. She worked so hard to make sure we knew she was there for us and loved us. So even though she traveled for work, I feel like we got more of a bonding experience because we were more of her focus when she was in town. I cherished the moments I had with her when she was home and never took her for granted, and I think that was really good for our relationship."

Both of Jody Camp's sons have birthdays in December, and so do she and her mom, so she devotes that month entirely to her family. "I decided after Brody, my second child, was born in December that December would be off limits to my friends and any holiday parties or Secret Santa at work," she says. "I don't do anything except circle the wagons and take care of my boys. I really want them to enjoy their birthdays, and I want to separate their birthdays from the crazy holiday season. So I take that month off from the parties and holiday lunches and gift exchanges with friends and devote my time to working and enjoying my family, but I step it up for the eleven other months to make up for it."

Summary

Guilt is a crushing emotion and a natural reaction when you're a working mom. I think the key to overcoming these feelings is for us to feel positive about what we're doing and not let the internal or external sources of guilt sabotage us. Instead of getting angry and frustrated about other people's traditional beliefs or ignorance, we can invest our energy into devising ways to keep the internal and external guilt from getting to us. You're a great mom doing a great job, so for your own health and sanity, get over it.

'I'm a Great Working Mom' Exercises

1. I want to or need to work outside the home because:

_____

_____

_____

_____

_____

_____

2. Things I love about my job:

_____

_____

_____

_____

_____

_____

_____

_____

_____

_____

3. How working makes me a better person and mom:

_____

_____

_____

_____

_____

_____

_____

_____

_____

4. How my kids and our family benefit from my job:

_____

_____

_____

_____

_____

_____

_____

_____

5. What I will say to people who question my decision to work outside the home:

_____

_____

_____

_____

_____

_____

_____

_____

_____

Sanity Savers

-   Remember that it's not possible for real women to be perfect moms or perfect employees.

-   Stop comparing yourself with stay-at-home moms.

-   Reflect on all the positive things about working outside the home.

-   Remember that no decision is perfect.

-   Do what it takes to feel good about being a working mom. By feeling positive about what we're doing, it's easier to stop the internal and external sources of guilt from sabotaging us.

STEP TWO

Setting Sane Expectations
There's No Such Thing as Balance!

I'm sure this scene will be familiar to you. It's nine o'clock at night. One of the kids has a birthday the next day and asked you to make cupcakes for the entire class of twenty-five. The boss dropped a last-minute assignment on you as you were leaving work and asked for it by noon tomorrow. Your partner would like to spend some time together. And the dog just threw up on the carpet.

I don't know how the concept of a "balanced life" for working moms began, but we need to put an end to this myth. We can certainly divide our time between work and family, but we can't be perfect moms, wives and workers all at the same time. We see other working moms who appear to have it all together and chastise ourselves for our weaknesses. We think we should be able to excel at all the roles we play every day. And we make ourselves crazy.

"I will be the perfect mom with perfect kids."

"I can maintain a balance between my work and my responsibilities as a mom."

"I can work out seven days a week."

"I can make this all work, every day".

Baloney. We can't. And it's time we stop trying.

An important step in becoming a sane working mom, a great mom, is accepting that we cannot do everything at 150 percent and survive the stress we place on ourselves by setting expectations that are too high in every aspect of our life. While it's frustrating to have other people impose unrealistic expectations on us, I think we're sometimes hardest on ourselves. When I was married to Dan, he didn't expect me to prepare homemade meals every day, but I felt like I should. If you're the creative type and enjoy making your kids' Halloween costumes and going all out with Christmas decorations, more power to you, but don't think any less of yourself if you don't have the energy or time to do those things.

Set Your Own Priorities

Prioritizing what's most important to us and letting go of the rest of it is an essential component of being sane working moms. A good friend of mine enjoyed doing theme parties for her kids' birthdays, and one year she went all out and threw a party with a Superman theme. Besides baking two cakes, she made Superman capes for all the boys and even made a life-size cardboard cutout of Superman that the boys could have their pictures taken with. Her son loved it, and she had fun doing it and felt good about it.

This is a great example of how one mom's pleasure is another mom's pain. This would have been torture for me. Needless to say, my son's birthday party that year was quite different. I let Holden pick out an inexpensive piñata and some decorations at a party shop. I bought plain brown lunch bags, markers and stickers and the kids all decorated the bags, excited about the next step: breaking open the piñata and using their bags to collect the candy. This party took only about an hour to plan, it was completely stress-free for me and the kids had a fantastic time.

Another year, Regan wanted to have a sleepover for her fifth birthday. I knew that most of the girls coming had never slept over at a friend's house, and I came up with a simple way to make them feel at home. Regan and I cut squares out of an old pink flannel sheet and sewed (inexpertly!) doll-size sleeping bags. We bought fabric markers, paint and sequins and invited each girl to bring her favorite doll to the party. Before dinner, we spread out the doll sleeping bags and the materials, and the girls really enjoyed decorating the sleeping bags. We let them dry during dinner and a short movie, and then we tucked all the girls into their sleeping bags and all their dolls into *their* sleeping bags. The parents were shocked the next day when not one girl had called in the middle of the night wanting to come home! And it hadn't been a huge effort. I think dinner was take-out and the cake was store-bought.

We all lie awake at night thinking about how we can make a birthday party more special or a work report more scintillating. But we need to be realistic about our skills and available time and not feel guilty if we don't have the extra hour to turn our monthly reports into spellbinding presentations, don't have it in us to throw the perfect party or aren't skillful wizards in the kitchen. Good is good enough. I've learned that myself as I've turned in papers for my PhD program that I wished I'd had a few more hours to perfect. But writing a proposal for work and having dinner with my daughter took precedence. We do the best we can every day in each of our roles.

"After several 'I'm not Betty Crocker' baking events, I bought cookies and cupcakes at a nice bakery instead of staying up late making them," says Shannon Oury, executive director of the Lawrence-Douglas County Housing Authority in Kansas. "You work all day, come home, do dinner, drive around for soccer and whatnot, and then if there's a party at school the next day, you need to make two dozen cupcakes. I just never could pull that off after everything else. Plus I really have no great cooking or baking skills. One day we were all supposed to make cookies for a school trip to the pumpkin patch. Mine turned out totally flat and I said, 'I'm not doing this anymore.'"

Working moms are typically spread very thin. We don't have time to whip up gourmet feasts on a regular basis or host five-course dinner parties. We don't write notes on each of our holiday cards. We don't make our kids' Halloween costumes each year. And we're okay with that! Each of us has things that we enjoy doing that are time-consuming, such as cooking and creating party decorations, but we mustn't pressure ourselves with the "keep up with the Joneses" mentality of doing it all, either at home or at work. "Just do what works for you and try not to compare," as Gloria Bokenkamp, donor relations and stewardship specialist at the University of Denver, says.

And as Ruby says, "Just realize that you're not perfect. You can't do everything, you can't be everywhere. But as long as you give your all at whatever you're doing, you're doing the best you can do. I used to help my daughter with her math homework, but she told me she got it wrong when I helped her. I felt bad, but she just laughed."

Before my kids were born, I worked sixty to seventy hours a week and was one of the highest achievers in my company. Now I work fifty to sixty hours a week. Things fall through the cracks at times and I leave work every day knowing that there are at least twenty more things I should have accomplished, but I know deep in my heart that I'm working hard, that I'm productive at work, and that I'm doing the best job I can given the time constraints I have. Being the president of a company is a responsibility that I take very seriously, and I'm committed to the success of our organization and the people who work for me. And my company continues to value me, not just for my achievements at work but also for being a loving mom to my kids.

Over the years I've learned that allowing our kids to not be perfect at everything all the time is as important as letting go of our own perfectionism. When we repainted Regan's bedroom when she was thirteen and I asked her what pictures she'd like to hang, she said, "None." That will look odd, I thought to myself, but that's what she wanted, and it was her room. Her choice wasn't going to endanger anyone, so I nodded, smiled and said, "OK." And it truly was fine. No one was judging me or her for not hanging any pictures on her wall. Years later she bought her first piece of art, a beautiful large piece, and it was finally the right time to hang something on her wall!

"Gretchen's dedication to our firm's success is clear in her preparation, organization and effort. At the same time, her passion for her children and family is present in all that she does. As the father of two young kids, I appreciate the example Gretchen sets for service to our firm while stressing the importance of family in all of our lives."

—Clark Ellis, Founder and Principal, Continuum Advisory Group

There are dozens of little things we can either anguish over or let go, but the more we're willing to let them go, the saner we can be. This is especially important to remember on those rare occasions when we can't come through for our kids. Lucy, a single, working mom, says she felt terrible when she couldn't afford to buy a lunch box for her daughter, who was starting kindergarten. "She really wanted a lunch box and she wanted to bring her own lunch. It really got to me that I couldn't do it for her. I convinced her that it was OK for her to eat the hot lunch the first day, and the next day I got the money and took her to the store to pick out the lunch box she wanted."

Sharon Knight, president and CEO of Warren Village, says, "I always set high expectations for myself, and there were a few times when they were clearly unattainable. I did a lot of deep analysis to determine the most important goals for both work and home. I looked for things I could let go so I could put more energy into the projects or activities that were most important. I accomplished fewer tasks, but everything I did complete was done better." Wise words!

Delegate as Much as You Can

There are certain things that we each decide we really want to do for our kids and at our jobs, and those are the things we should hold on to. Everything else on our lists should be up for review. And just like with letting go of the little things, the more we can delegate—to our kids, to someone we hire, to our partners—the saner we'll be. We don't have to do it all ourselves!

Traveling taught me a valuable lesson about this. Just because someone is doing it in a way that's different from the way I would do it doesn't make it wrong. Because I traveled so much, I had to accept that Dan, my mom, my sister and the kids' caregivers would do things differently from how I would. It took effort at times, though. I remember coming home from a trip to find Holden with his diaper on backward—but it was on! I also learned that if it was really important to control a certain thing while I was gone, I could figure out a way to do it. I didn't want my kids to drink too much juice, and instead of trying to police how much they had, I just told the caregivers "no juice," period, for the first two years. My kids didn't know what they were missing, and I didn't have to worry that bottles of juice were rotting their teeth.

Gloria Bokenkamp says that when her three children were in their teens, her husband worked out of state after losing his job in the mortgage industry in the 2008 crash. He was gone two weeks at a time and she was working full time, taking care of three teenagers and trying to keep up with everything that had to be done every day. "A friend of mine said, 'You need to teach your kids to do their own laundry,'" Gloria says. "And I kind of thought, 'Oh, it's not a problem if I'm doing laundry anyway.' But finally I gave in and gave them a lesson on how to do laundry, and from then on they did it themselves. Delegating this one job was a lifesaver."

Making the Best of What We Have

One of the ways to help keep our expectations in check is to make the best of what we already have. Jeanne Saunders shared that after she divorced and bought a new house for herself and her daughters, she went to her storage unit to get her furniture and discovered that most of it had been stolen. "My daughters were three and five at the time," she says. "I bought beds and a couch, but we didn't have any other furniture and we didn't have a TV. It was right when the book *Harry Potter* came out and so I started reading out loud to them every night. And I can remember getting hoarse from reading for so long, but they'd plead, 'Read more, read more!' I loved those books, too, so I enjoyed it just as much as they did. It didn't matter that we didn't have a TV, because the girls loved the time we spent together. Another simple activity we enjoyed was to go for a walk after dinner. We'd get home from our walk, get in our jammies, get on the couch and read. It was good quality time together."

How to Set Sane Expectations

One way to set sane expectations for ourselves is to look at the various roles we play and decide on the really important goals for each role. Steven Covey, author of *The Seven Habits of Highly Effective People*, says that thinking about our lives as a combination of roles and defining goals for these roles is crucial. We also need to understand that the roles we juggle throughout our lives will change. For example, when my mom was in the last stages of Alzheimer's disease, my role as a daughter intensified. I had to give up something in another role and chose to take three months off from my role as "leader" to care for her. After she and my dad passed away, this role disappeared.

My current main roles are mom, girlfriend, president of Continuum Advisory Group, sister and friend. Every year I set goals for myself, in writing, for each of my roles. It helps me think about what's realistic to expect of myself, and it helps me to understand that I can't do 150 percent in every role all the time.

Here's an example of one of my annual roles-and-goals lists, from a couple of years ago:

- Mom – When I'm with my kids, be "present" and not thinking about work. Once a week do something with the kids that they enjoy doing. Make sure they are eating nutritious home-cooked meals.

- Girlfriend – Be certain to carve out time for Philip (his language of love is quality time!) no matter how busy I am, including weekend trips nearly every month.

- Ex-wife – Work hard to communicate effectively with Dan and to be good parents to our kids; make sure we meet twice a year to discuss the kids.

- President – Run the company effectively, achieve my goals and have happy employees and clients.

- Sibling – Take at least three trips to Kansas City each year to see Kurt. Be supportive of Pam and spend time with her each month.

- Friend – Be there for my friends when they need me; do two fun things with friends each month

- PhD student – Be present in class and respectful of my classmates; complete my assignments on time and at least at a "B" level (this is hard to accept, but I can't do everything perfectly).

Focusing on What's Important to You

Making my annual list helps me focus on what's most important to me and what isn't that important. For example, I wanted my kids to have great birthday cakes, but cake-baking is on my "not important to do myself" list. Fortunately, I didn't have to bake them myself because I found Cakes by Karen, a wonderful bakery that made them for me. My daughter is also a talented cake-maker, and for the past few years she's taken it on herself to create gorgeous birthday cakes for all of us.

On the other hand, making sure the kids have a home-cooked dinner is on my "important" list, so I had to figure out how to do that. (They might say they wish I hadn't been quite so successful with this goal and that eating dinner out would have been better!) To accomplish this goal, I frequently cooked all the food for the week on Sunday so that it could just be heated up throughout the week when I don't have time to cook. Before the kids were in college, it wasn't unusual for me to have all six burners on the stove going on Sunday. This might sound awful to someone who doesn't like to cook, but I enjoy doing it because it's important to me.

Find Out What Others Expect

In addition to setting sane expectations for ourselves, we need to have open and honest conversations with our kids, partners and employers so we know what they expect. We may not always be able to meet those expectations, but we can try and we can also create compromises. It's up to us to open the dialogue and find out what's most important to them. If we have only a couple of hours to devote to our kids on a weekend, we might assume it's most important to them that we attend their hockey game when they'd actually rather spend those two hours having pizza with us and hanging out. Their expectations change as they grow and change, so leave an opening for your kids to update you on what's most important to them at any given time.

Shannon Oury shared that one of her daughters recently challenged her about being more authentic. "I realized that I had spent so much time 'doing' for them and around them that, in the rush and desire to make things 'perfect' for them, I hadn't shared who I really am with them, flaws and all," she says. "Now that they're becoming women I'm trying to be more real with them and less the perfect mom.

We also want to be sure we understand what our employers expect and have clearly defined goals for our roles at work. I have tried to work with each of my direct supervisors to define boundaries and expectations that work for both the company and me, given the other demands on my life. When I accepted the position in San Francisco as chief philanthropic engagement officer for the Women's Funding Network (WFN), my boss, President and CEO Chris Grumm, and I defined the expectations: I'd be in San Francisco every other week and do a manageable amount of travel beyond that. We also defined performance expectations. When I decided to take some time off to be with my mom, who was in the last stages of Alzheimer's and spend time with my kids, who were both in high school, I worked with my partners at Continuum Advisory Group to create a COO position that would allow me to work half time and achieve a defined set of objectives for the company. After my mom passed away, I accepted the position of president and set boundaries around special occasions and worked out my travel schedule so that my daughter could live with me every other week. Sometimes that didn't work perfectly. My ex-husband has been very flexible in accommodating my work-travel schedule, and Regan has always understood that I need to make a living and that exceptions to this rule will happen. Now she understands that I'm a single mom putting three people through college.

Find Realistic Ways to Volunteer at School

Because it was hard for me to volunteer at my kids' schools during the week, I tried to find other ways to be involved. I was the team manager and treasurer for their hockey teams nearly every year. Try keeping track of thousands of dollars for two teams simultaneously—talk about confusing! But it was something I could do late at night, and it made good use of my finance and organizational skills.

Setting boundaries and expectations is important even as a volunteer. I asked the team members' parents, "Please don't e-mail me on my personal e-mail at 3 p.m. on Friday afternoon asking where the game is that night. I have a full-time job and I don't check my personal e-mail during the day." One day a dad walked up to me and said, "You really do have a full-time job! I saw you on CNN talking about the Women's Foundation of Colorado." He viewed me as a "hockey mom," not as a business leader. Funny how people have paradigms based on the context they know you in!

Dan and I also chaired the annual giving campaign at the Montessori School of Denver and Cherry Hills Village Elementary, where we raised $140,000 for textbooks and technology. Once again, it leveraged my skills, contributed to the school and made me feel good. It was work that I could do mostly at night and on weekends, although on occasion there were planning meetings at the swimming pool, where I was the only person in a business suit.

Celebrate the Successes—Big and Small

As my friend Jody Camp says, "I just know that I'm lucky if one part of my life 'wins' on any given day. Sometimes I kick ass at work and have an amazing professional day. Sometimes I rule at Chuck E. Cheese and my kids give me hugs unprompted. And sometimes I actually get a mani/pedi and I win that day. I don't have false expectations that I can balance everything every day."

And I love the way Deidre Bacala put it: "It's impossible to be the best at work and at home. You'll make yourself crazy trying. Just know that some days you'll be a rockin' mom and some days you'll be a stellar employee, but rarely, if ever, on the same day!"

When we working moms share our authentic experiences and challenges with each other, we find out that we're not the only one who's struggling to keep all the balls in the air. "The best thing I ever did was to be very open and honest with my friends in similar situations," says Leslie Mitchell, retired president of FirstBank of Cherry Creek, Colorado. "I think we actually make things worse for all working women when we try to act as if everything is perfect and we can do it all without consequences. Real conversations with friends made me realize that I wasn't the only one who felt that she was failing at everything and succeeding at nothing." So talk to your friends about what your reality looks like and your struggles and challenges. If we all learn to be vulnerable with each other, we will all benefit.

Summary

I don't know you, but since you're reading this book, I know you're a great mom. You care about your kids. You care about your work. You care about your family, your friends, and the world in general. Do yourself a favor: be easier on yourself. Pat yourself on the back. Understand what you can and can't do. And be happy—you deserve it!

'I'm a Great Working Mom' Exercises

1. What do other moms do that makes me feel inferior?

_____

_____

_____

_____

_____

_____

_____

_____

_____

2. What can I do to feel better about myself and my expectations of myself?

_____

_____

_____

_____

_____

_____

_____

3. When am I too hard on myself?

_____

_____

_____

_____

_____

_____

_____

_____

4. What are my primary "roles" in life?

_____

_____

_____

_____

_____

_____

_____

_____

5. What are my goals for each role for this year?

_____

_____

_____

_____

_____

_____

_____

_____

6. What can I stop doing that will make my life simpler and easier?

_____

_____

_____

_____

_____

_____

_____

_____

_____

Sanity Savers

- Remember that we cannot maintain a perfect balance between work and motherhood.

- Prioritize what's most important to you and let go of the rest. The more we're willing to let them go, the saner we can be.

- Make the best of what you already have.

- Ask our kids what they need most from you.

- Talk to your friends about our reality, struggles and challenges.

- Remind yourself, "I'm doing a great job. Lighten up."

STEP THREE

Fix Your Job
(And Your Partner's Too)
Shaping Your Job to Fit Your Family

One year I almost missed our annual Fourth of July trip to visit family in Kansas City because of a potential new client. I had someone working on the proposal, but he was new and couldn't finish it on his own, particularly since much of the knowledge for the proposal resided in my head. I was determined to find a way to keep the Fourth of July tradition, so I collaborated with my colleague by cell phone. Thankfully, he was willing to put up with the fact that the calls happened in 15-minute segments as I passed through towns in Kansas that had cell-phone reception. Every time I got close to a town, I'd call him and talk until I lost reception. Then I'd call him again as I approached the next town. This went on for nine hours! That was my way of not canceling the family trip and still meeting my work obligations. As the saying goes, where there's a will, there's a way! We just have to find it.

Those of us who were workaholics before we had kids usually have a harder time cutting back on work. Women are often driven to succeed and put in long hours, especially when we're competing in male-dominated fields and believe we need to do more than our male counterparts to be successful. Before my kids were born, I traveled three or four days a week, regularly worked until seven at night, and worked half of almost every Saturday. I was your typical overachiever and took on every responsibility at work that was given to me. I cut back when the kids were born, but the transformation didn't happen overnight. I had to make up my own version of the twelve-step program to make a clean break from my work addiction.

The first step was, "Learn to say no." I had to accept that I was not Wonder Woman and could not be everything to everyone, including my employer. I didn't have to explain, rationalize or make up excuses anymore. I could simply say no or "no, thank you."

Easier said than done, though. I learned how to say no the hard way when my son Holden was nine months old and I was eighteen weeks' pregnant with Regan. I had just gotten home from a checkup for Holden and suddenly felt as if my water had broken. I rushed to the bathroom and was terrified when I saw that I was bleeding. My hands were shaking as I called my doctor, and she told me to drive to the hospital immediately. The ultrasound showed that I had placenta previa and was hemorrhaging. I was hospitalized for a day and then sent home and told to rest until the bleeding stopped, which it did the next day. But as soon as I went back to work, I started bleeding again. I was so shaken that I scraped the side of my car on a dumpster in our alley as I pulled into the garage. My doctor told me the only way I could keep my baby was to lie almost flat on my back all day every day until the bleeding stopped completely. I could raise myself up to only a thirty-degree angle in bed, and I could shower twice a week and use the bathroom. That was it.

For an entire month, that's what I did. Let me tell you, there's no way to work on a laptop while you're on your back. It's even hard to sound intelligent on the phone. And so I took a month off and I watched a lot of movies.

My work team rallied and was entirely supportive and understanding. Afterward, many of my friends who understand my Type A nature asked, "How could you possibly have handled lying flat on your back for a month?" My response? "If the doctor tells you that the only way to save your baby is to lie flat on your back until the bleeding stops, you lie flat on your back for a month." Work survived, I survived and Regan survived to be the beautiful young woman she is today.

How to Fix Your Job

If just reading the words *how to fix your job* made you uneasy, you're in good company. There are millions of women who are making significant contributions at work but don't feel comfortable asking for changes in their schedules or duties when they have kids. It makes me sad that women—and men, for that matter—often don't see the true value we bring to the workplace or feel worthy of asking for "rule changes" that allow us to spend more time with our families.

After the birth of my second child, I asked my manager if I could arrange my travel schedule so that I was spending only two nights a week away from home. My husband and I had discussed how much travel we both could tolerate, so this was a joint decision. My manager quickly agreed. He would rather have me working full time and traveling two nights a week than not have me working at all.

A friend of mine who was working full time as an attorney wanted to go to a four-day workweek but was afraid to make that request. She worked harder than anyone I knew, and I couldn't imagine that her employers would risk losing her, one of their top performers. When she finally worked up the nerve to ask, they said yes immediately.

So if you're nervous about asking for an adjustment in your work schedule or changes in your responsibilities, summon the courage to ask. The worst thing that can happen is that they say no.

I realize this isn't easy. Two years after I cut my travel back to two nights a week, I switched to reporting to a different manager. The first time I sent him performance review factors, he vehemently questioned my choice to travel just two nights a week. "I'm not certain that you can be successful in your position with that schedule," he said.

"Do you think I've been successful for the past two years?" I asked him.

"Yes," he said, and that's when I told him that I'd been traveling only two nights a week for the past two years. He was surprised that I'd found ways to keep my billings high without traveling extensively.

Being successful doesn't always mean working harder. It often means working smarter.

Adjust Your Work Schedule

Sometimes adjusting your work schedule simply means arriving earlier, working later or doing some work at home. These small adjustments can make major differences if you need to drop your kids off at day care or school on your way to work or pick them up at the end of the day. Having some flexibility with your hours will give you the breathing room you need when your baby-sitter or caregiver calls in sick, when your kids have accidents or get sick and you have to leave work to pick them up, and any time something unexpected happens—which is frequently when we have kids!

Sometimes you need to make bigger adjustments. Robin was employed as a school-bus driver, but when she had kids and had to be at work by 6 a.m., the schedule didn't work for her. She felt good about the day care her kids were in, but it didn't open until 7 a.m. She knew the school couldn't change its schedule, so she found a new job, working for a car rental company. Her manager allows her flexibility in her schedule so she can work forty hours a week and still get her kids to day care. Shannon Oury left her position as corporate council for Johns Manville to work part-time teaching law at the University of Kansas until her youngest was in first grade. Lisa Walker took her kids to work with her until they were five months old. Rachel Contizano, an AmeriCorps VISTA member, took a summer off to spend more time with her son before he started kindergarten. Lora Ledermann cut back to part-time hours when her first child was born.

"I'm still part-time today, and I've never regretted a minute of it," she says. "I've given several moms at my office the same part-time opportunity because I think it will be the success of our future."

My friend Betsy Mordecai, who refers to herself as "Queen of Quite a Lot" at MorEvents Inc., changed her schedule when her son started middle school so she could be home when he got home from school every day and drive him to activities. Jody Camp has arranged flex time so she can leave the office in time to pick up her kids at school one day a week. "I get into work on those days at six thirty so one day a week my kids get to stand with all the other kids in the car line, and they're puffed up like little peacocks when they get to jump into Mommy's car instead of going to aftercare," she says.

Back to the External Guilt

When my kids were two and three, I took a two-month sabbatical to be with them full time. It went so well that I did it again when the kids were five and six. Both times I planned for the sabbatical six months in advance so that it would go smoothly, without my having to rearrange speaking engagements or have a negative impact on my clients or my team. I did it because I wanted my kids to know that they were just as important to me as my job.

The people who worked for me knew they could contact me in an emergency, but they handled everything themselves with grace and ease. To smooth the transition back to work, I planned it so that my kids went back to preschool and kindergarten the same day I went back to work. They were excited about going back to school and, truth be told, probably ready for Mom to go back to work!

Not everyone was supportive of the decisions I made. At the time of my second sabbatical, I was a shareholder in the company and agreed to one trip during my sabbatical, to Raleigh, North Carolina, for our annual shareholder meeting and my presentation of my unit's business plan for the upcoming fiscal year. Several shareholders were on a direct flight together on a small regional jet from Denver to Raleigh, an experience I've described as being a bit like being shoved into a beer can and flown across the country. Early in the flight, a shareholder sitting across the aisle from me said, "Must be nice to take eight weeks off."

"It's important to me that my kids know that Mom can go eight weeks without getting on a plane and that they're as important to me as my work," I said.

"If you thought your work was important, you wouldn't feel the need to take time off from it," he replied.

I was shocked and furious. How dare he imply that work wasn't important to me when I spent a portion of every week away from my family for it? I was worried that I would be arrested for murdering someone on a plane! Instead, I said, "You know, we're all really bright people. As long as all thirty-six directors don't take the same eight weeks off, we could probably figure out how to give everyone a sabbatical."

Changing Your Responsibilities or Your Job

Sometimes, adjusting your schedule isn't possible or isn't enough and you need to change your job responsibilities. This might mean swapping responsibilities with someone in your department temporarily or permanently. It could also mean moving from one position to another. When my kids were six and seven, I handed over the consulting business unit I was running to someone else and took over our research group. Because the research group was located in Raleigh, I spent one week a month there, but the arrangement allowed me to stay home for most of the rest of the month and I was still able to make a significant impact on the growth of that business unit.

Sometimes changing jobs is a necessity, and that usually isn't easy. It can even mean that you need to have new training or education to make the kind of change that you need. Deidre Bacala changed jobs and took a salary reduction because "the schedule and demands were not working for our family," she says. "I miss the work and my colleagues but wouldn't trade it for the world for a more relaxed work schedule. A happy mommy equals a happy family!"

Shannon Oury says, "I downshifted my career and moved to a small town where school, soccer practice and my kids' other activities were five to ten minutes from work. It made it possible for me to work and to be at most events, coach soccer and volunteer at school."

Before Jody Camp and her husband decided it was time to start their family, Jody had been program manager for Water for People for almost seven years, traveling the world five or more months a year and working in Honduras, Guatemala, Kenya, and India and wherever else her development work took her. "My husband had a consulting job where he traveled the country," she says, "and all of the sudden he was like, 'Wait, I can't do this anymore.' I said, 'Hell, no, you can't, because I'm not a single mom.' So both my husband and I had to readjust and rethink what our careers looked like and our ability to travel or our inability to travel. I know a lot of women and men that continue to travel for work after having their babies. And that's great and wonderful and it works for them. That's just not what Shad and I wanted for our family.

"Since my husband and I both had jet-set, go-getting careers, it took us quite a while to settle into working near home and managing a family. But that's what we both wanted. We want to have all four family members as an essential part of the day-to-day workings of our lifestyle. But the transition didn't happen overnight. It actually took me a few years to settle into this new way of living. Instead of grabbing my bags and flying out to Kenya, I was grabbing my kids' diaper bags and heading out to day care."

When I was president of the Women's Foundation of Colorado, I hired Jody as our director of programs, which was her first job after Water for People. She was an incredible asset to our team and we became great friends. Since I was also a working mom, I was glad I had the opportunity to give Jody the flexibility she needed when she became pregnant and had her two boys.

When my own kids were seven and eight, I decided I didn't want to travel as much, and I really wanted to get to know my Denver community. I went back to night school for two years, while still traveling, to earn a master's in nonprofit management from Regis University. It was hard and took some of my time from the kids, but I knew it would allow me to make a transition to a job that didn't require so much travel. When I graduated, I became president and CEO of the Women's Foundation, where I spent five deeply fulfilling years and developed amazing relationships with the leaders of the Colorado community.

Six years later, newly divorced and commuting to San Francisco for my "dream job" as chief philanthropic officer for the Women's Funding Network, I decided that my mom and kids needed me to be back in Denver full time. Fortunately, I was recruited to return to Denver as assistant dean of the Daniels College of Business at the University of Denver. When the kids were a little older and my mom's health was failing, I changed jobs again and returned to management consulting and eventually accepted the position of president of Continuum Advisory Group to give me more flexibility in my schedule. Each of these job changes was scary in some ways, but I was making the move for the right reasons and was fortunate that it was possible to do so.

Protecting Your Vacation Time

Most of us don't get nearly enough vacation time, so we need to fiercely protect the time we have and use it wisely to spend quality time with our family or take care of ourselves with a break from the kids. Whether you go away for vacation or spend your vacation time at home, if possible make sure your employer knows you won't be available unless there's a true emergency. Resist the urge to call in to work. To the degree that you can, let the world turn without you.

During my first sabbatical, when the kids were two and three years old, we visited Grand Lake, Colorado. It was the first time I'd been there, and at first I was frustrated that my cell phone didn't work there. And then I had a "eureka" moment. *My cell phone doesn't work here!*

We went to Grand Lake for a week every summer after that!

I explained to my team members that completely disconnecting was important to me, that if they really had an emergency they could call me at the hotel, but they respected my need to get away and were fully capable of running the organization in my absence. There were times when being in touch couldn't be avoided, though. During one trip while I was president of the Women's

Foundation, we were wrapping up a $12 million campaign and finalizing the names of the donors to be etched in stone on a sculpture in recognition of their donations. It was important to my team for me to be in contact with my office once a day to support their decisions because these decisions were permanent! I discovered that if I stood on a certain rock about two feet into the lake I could get a couple of bars of reception on my cell. I no doubt looked like a crazy woman, standing on a rock surrounded by water and talking on my cell phone, but my team appreciated the help and I was ecstatic that I could do what needed to be done and not miss out on the vacation with my kids.

I know it isn't always possible to completely tune out on vacation, nor is it always desirable, but setting boundaries and limits regarding how much vacation time to devote to work is helpful. When the kids were ten and eleven, we went to Normandy and Paris during a particularly busy time at work, and spending an hour a day on e-mail was necessary and made the balance of my time on vacation relaxing because I knew I was taking care of business. So carve out a little time for work if you must, but make sure that opening the door a crack doesn't result in a deluge of work. Explain to your kids why it is important that you work – they understand.

And then there are situations where your work is a labor of love and vacation is a great time to focus on it. I've written and edited most of this book while on vacation— in Grand Lake, Hawaii and Lake of the Ozarks in 2014 and Australia in 2015. It truly is a labor of love, and my family and friends understand my need to carve out a couple of hours every morning to write.

Involve Your Kids in Work

I also involve my kids in my work whenever it's appropriate. While I was working at the Women's Foundation and my kids were in middle school, they were assigned the job of working with our team to collect the giving envelopes from the twenty-six hundred people who attended our annual fundraising luncheon. By taking part in the luncheon, they were also able to meet our guest speakers, including Cokie Roberts, Jehan Sadat, Lisa Ling and Joy Behar. It was a great experience for them and they were able to see firsthand the impact I had on our community. When I was assistant dean at the University of Denver, Regan and Holden attended many alumni and donor events. By the time they were fifteen and sixteen, when we'd arrive at an event, they were completely comfortable socializing and networking on their own. One of my proudest "great mom" moments was when one of our alumni said my kids were two of the most articulate people he'd spoken to that evening. It's fun to involve them in my work, and they benefit from the experience, learning to network and meeting interesting people.

Parenting Is a Partnership

These suggestions and strategies for reshaping your job also apply to your partners. Many women assume that they need to adjust their work schedule but don't think about their partners' making adjustments at work, too. When the kids were young and I was out of town, my husband would take our kids to school and work from 9 a.m. to 6 p.m. instead of 8 a.m. to 5 p.m. I've never known a job that couldn't be adjusted in some way to more closely align with your needs. Most employers are thrilled to have hard-working, productive, results-oriented employees and will work with you to find the parameters that meet your needs. Making these decisions about your work and your partner's work has to be done together. Being unified in your decisions will add strength to your parenting relationship.

Accept That There Are No Perfect Decisions

These work-related decisions are all difficult because no matter what we choose to do, we will experience benefits and drawbacks. That's why it's critical for us to make these important decisions based on our own personal needs and the needs of our families. There is no "right" answer. If my end goal in life had been to make as much money as I could, to maximize my financial success in life, I would have made different choices. Had I not had kids, I would have made different choices. But I did have kids and I'm happy with the choices I've made because I was being true to myself and to my kids with each choice. Being a mom is the most fulfilling relationship in my life.

The more we can be true to ourselves and our loved ones, the fewer regrets we're likely to have, but that doesn't mean we won't experience moments when we question our decisions. When Regan was two, I took her to my office for the first time. When we got there and I showed her around, she asked, "Where's your bed?"

It took me a few minutes to realize that when I traveled she thought I was sleeping at my office. I felt horrible that my daughter thought I was sleeping ten minutes away instead of coming home. I wracked my brain to think of a way to help her and Holden understand that Mommy got on an airplane and went far away to do her work, and finally I came up with the idea to buy a large United States map that was mounted on corrugated board and came with little pushpin flags. Each week before I left town, I would lift the kids up and stick pins in the cities I was going to. I'm not sure when they finally realized that these were far-away places, but it helped me feel like I was doing something to help them understand why I couldn't come home every night.

Changing the Way Leaders and Corporations Treat Working Parents

It's up to us to help educate leaders and corporations about the strain of working and being a parent. We need to educate companies about how to create a culture where women feel comfortable making decisions and adjustments that work for themselves, the company and the family. Jeanne Saunders, having worked for many large organizations, set a good example for other leaders by allowing the women who worked for her to modify their work schedules so they could be home earlier in the afternoon.

There are many other enlightened business leaders who do what they can to support the women in their organizations who are raising kids, but we need many, many more leaders like this. If each of us has the courage to ask for the flexibility and adjustments that we need at work, we can raise awareness of these needs for all women.

Summary

We all want to be successful. We work hard to be great moms and great employees. Don't be afraid to explore different schedules or work opportunities that are a better fit. It will reduce your stress and help you to stay a great mom.

'I'm a Great Working Mom' Exercises

1. What responsibilities have I taken on that are outside my job duties and need to be dropped?

_____

_____

_____

_____

_____

_____

_____

_____

_____

_____

_____

_____

_____

_____

2. What is a reasonable work schedule that works for my partner and child-care provider and will give me the time I need and want with my kids?

_____

_____

_____

_____

_____

_____

_____

3. What does my work schedule need to be to fit with my child care?

_____

_____

_____

_____

_____

_____

_____

4. How should I approach my company about changes I would like to make?

_____

_____

_____

_____

_____

_____

_____

5. What are my options if my employer won't allow me to change my schedules/duties/etc.?

_____

_____

_____

_____

_____

_____

_____

_____

_____

Sanity Savers

- If we're afraid to ask for an adjustment in our work schedule, we need to summon the courage to ask anyway.

- Remember that "No" is a complete sentence and an acceptable response.

- If adjusting our schedule isn't enough, we need to change our job responsibilities or our jobs.

- Protect your vacation time and use it wisely for yourself and your family.

- Help leaders and corporations to understand the strain of working and being a parent.

STEP FOUR

Building a Child-Rearing Partnership
The 'Uber' Team

I remember agonizing over whether to give my kids the chickenpox vaccination, which was new at the time they were born. Little did I know that this was one of about a million decisions I would make for my kids before they turned eighteen!

These types of decisions are a lot easier when you have someone to lean on, someone who is committed to helping you to be a great mom. Many of my friends have quit their jobs because of the stress of working while having little or no help at home. I can't even imagine having raised my kids without a partner, one primary person who's there for me and my kids through thick and thin.

Having a partner to help you raise wonderful kids isn't about being married or being single. I know a lot of married women whose significant others are not their partners when it comes to raising the kids, and I know a lot of single moms who have fantastic partners who help them raise wonderful kids.

For nineteen years I was blessed with a loving husband who was a great partner in the business of raising great kids, but our partnership didn't happen by accident. It took a lot of hard work on both our parts, and it was definitely a roller coaster at times. Having kids puts a strain on all the relationships in your life. You've never done this before, and you're trying to do it "right" for the sake of yourself and your kids, creating a path to happiness and success for them and juggling all the new responsibilities that go hand in hand with having kids. Even the best partnerships are strained by the changes that need to be made when you have kids. Dan and I have been divorced for several years now, and I'm grateful that we have a strong friendship and that he's still my primary partner in raising the kids. Fortunately, we both put our kids first.

As a working mom, if you're trying to do everything related to child-rearing on your own—buying the clothes, caring for the kids when they're sick, filling out school paperwork—not only will it cause a lot of stress in your life, but if you have a significant other, you'll probably begin to resent him or her. Whether you're single or in a committed relationship, having a "partner" in this business of raising great kids will do wonders for your sanity. It may be your life partner, but sometimes it just doesn't work out that way.

Parenting Partnerships Take Many Forms

Figuring out how you want your child-rearing partnership to work is as individualized as it gets. What works great for one partnership may be disastrous in another. Just like there's no point in comparing ourselves with stay-at-home moms, there's no point in comparing our partnership with anyone else's. The secret to staying sane is to give serious consideration to what works best for your kids, you and your partner.

Jody Camp works close to her kids' school, so she can drop them off in about eight minutes. The challenge is that if she did the drop-off and pick up every day, she couldn't go into the office early or stay late. So her husband handles a few of the drop-offs or pickups every week. "Shad takes a bus downtown and it takes him about five minutes to get to work," Jody says. "When he has to do drop-off or pick up the boys, he has to drive the opposite way twenty minutes, come back twenty minutes, and then hop on that bus. It's a huge burden for him, but I need him to do it so that I can work late and go in early sometimes. Even if I don't have to work late or go in early, I ask him do it a couple days out of the week. It gives me a little bit of a break. I need my quiet time and I need my ability to connect with my boss and staff past five o'clock. Getting those breaks goes a long way! It means I'm not the one driving them home from aftercare every day when the boys are exhausted and bored and chucking goldfish crackers at the driver's head."

Dan and I chose all the kids' schools and caregivers together, some of the most important decisions of their lives. When I was in town, I took the kids to school and stayed home with them when they were sick. If I was out of town, Dan had that responsibility. I bought their clothes and did the grocery shopping, and Dan paid the bills and coached hockey and soccer. Sometimes we swapped jobs or did more than our share because one of us was busier than usual or just needed a tiny break. Having a conversation about responsibility and partnership is difficult, especially if one person believes they're bearing more of the burden than the other, but talking about it is an important first step.

Here are some other stories from my friends and colleagues:

"My 'primary partner' is my mom. She's one of the only people I trust with my son, she has the same rearing qualities I do, she has made sure to have a safe environment for my son (he has severe nut allergies) and she is a very loving grandma."

—Rachel Contizano

"My husband was an active, fully invested father from the time our kids were born. Fortunately, this was something we were on the same page about from the beginning. When he'd get home from work, he would take over to give me a break and do the baths and bedtime routines for all three kids!"

—Gloria Bokenkamp

"My sister and I have a great arrangement. It's all about give and take. I take care of her kids and she pays me by helping me to do things like get a computer for school with tax money. And when her kids wanted to take music lessons, I gave her a guitar and a violin to thank her for the favors she does for me."

—Shelly, single working mom

"We were fortunate that my husband could work four ten-hour days and have Fridays off, so he had Daddy day at home and I could go to the office on Fridays. It was the best thing for us all. He learned what it was like to be home with the kids, and he (had a closer relationship with them because of that). We have mutual expectations."

—Lora Ledermann

"My partner shares all responsibilities with raising our son, Stone. But I do the scheduling, signing up for activities and setting appointments because I feel better knowing firsthand that it's all getting done. He shares in the delivery."

—Betsy Mordecai

"I trade child care and taking kids to school with a friend who's also in school. She takes my daughter and her daughters to school on Mondays and Wednesdays and I take the girls on Tuesdays and Thursdays. We alternate on Fridays."

—Lucy, single working mom

"My husband is self-employed with a thriving business. We had to find the balance of two working parents and the household duties. He's on daddy duty two mornings a week, and I take care of the kids the other three mornings. We trade off picking the kids up. Each day is different based on our activities and schedule."

—Deidre Bacala

Finding a Partner

If you're not in a relationship with someone who is devoted to helping you, consider asking a family member or friend to be your child-rearing partner. You may think that sounds like a difficult role to propose to someone, but many people would be flattered to help, especially those who have experienced the challenges of raising kids themselves. You might try an approach like this: "I realize that I really need the support of a good friend to help me raise a great child. I'm looking for someone who will help me with decisions, spend some time with the kids and perhaps help out when they're sick so that I can go to work. They love you, look up to you and will realize that you played an essential role in their turning out to be great people." That's just a draft of an idea, but it will get you pointed in the right direction.

If all else fails and you don't have and can't find a primary partner, don't despair. The next chapter is all about creating a support network of resources that can help take the place of that primary partner. While it helps to have a "go-to" person you can rely on, having many hands works, too. As Hillary Clinton said, "It takes a village."

Steps to Ensure a Strong Child-Rearing Partnership

A true partnership begins with respect—respecting each other as individuals with needs beyond the role of parent. It's difficult to balance each other's needs, and it won't be perfect all the time, but hard work and *very open communication* are the building blocks.

The following steps may help you to get there:

1. Communicate frequently with your partner about your roles and who's doing what so that fewer things fall through the cracks. Decide who's doing the grocery shopping, paying the bills, helping with school projects, dropping off and picking the kids up from school and everything else that has to be done to keep your family operating smoothly.

2. Be open to making adjustments to your duties and responsibilities as your life changes or just for the sake of switching things up so that you're not always handling all the same responsibilities.

3. Make sure that you and your partner have clarity about your expectations and that neither of you are feeling more burdened than the other. Keep in mind that no matter how hard you try to divide things up equally, it's difficult to do without one person feeling as if they're doing more than the other.

4. Devote quality time to talking through decisions about important aspects of the kids' lives, such as child care, choice of schools and health care, to make sure you're on the same page and making important decisions together. This will lead to better decisions and help relieve anxiety about making the "wrong" decision.

Tips if You're Divorced

When we divorced, our kids were thirteen and fourteen years old, and it was a difficult decision for both of us. We attended counseling for six months before telling our kids because we wanted to be in as healthy a place as possible and there were certain decisions regarding the kids that we wanted to make before we told them. Handling it this way helped to reduce the stress and trauma that kids experience when their parents split up. We work hard to maintain a strong relationship as parents, and it's totally worth it.

We communicate frequently and have put the interest of our kids before our own interests both as individuals and as a divorced couple. We hosted joint Thanksgiving and Christmas celebrations with our kids and families when the kids were in high school. We bent over backward to create a living and vacation schedule that worked for the kids and for both of us. And we're flexible. For example, I was supposed to have the kids every other fall break, but Dan traditionally takes the kids to Florida to help his parents open their house, so for three years he had every fall break with the kids. I visit my family in Kansas City at the Fourth of July, so Dan let me have that holiday with the kids every year. We're both committed to our kids, and having a good working partnership was important to both of us.

Sharon Knight's son was five when she and her husband divorced, and she was committed to making sure her son had the opportunity to develop a good relationship with his father. "It was important for me to cement the value of family," she says. "I also wanted to spend as much time with my son as I could, so if I was going to go out on a date or do something with friends, it was a priority to try to do it when Jake was at his dad's house." Sharon says the most important part of making parenting work with her ex-husband was checking and double-checking all their arrangements. "It was essential to write everything down and double-check, because the worst thing that could possibly happen is if I thought Jake's dad was taking him somewhere and then all of a sudden I find out that Jake is stranded. We clearly delineated schedules, often months in advance, to accommodate work travel, teacher conferences, weekend trips, and everything else we had to fit in. It didn't always work out, but being that intentional was very, very important to all of us."

There's no doubt that keeping close track of all the details is a sanity saver. (I'll share some organizational tips in Step Seven.)

Summary

I'm so fortunate to have a child-rearing partner who respects my work and supports me as a great mom. My mom was also a great partner to us, doing things like giving us advice and driving the kids to preschool. Doing it alone is difficult, and we all need people to lean on. I hope this chapter helps you build your partnership.

'I'm a Great Working Mom' Exercises

1. Who is your childrearing partner?

   _____

   _____

2. How much time do you devote each week to parenting? (This includes making meals, doing laundry, driving kids to school or other activities, helping with homework, making beds, and spending time with your kids.)

   _____

   _____

3. How many hours do you work each week?

   _____

   _____

4. How many hours of help each week would be ideal?

   _____

   _____

5. What is the fewest number of hours you can manage with?

   _____

   _____

Now that you have a clear idea of just how much help you need, you can start thinking about who you would like to partner with, not just to get the extra hands-on help but also to have a partner in decision-making.

Creating the Child Rearing Partnership

1. Clearly write down your expectations of your primary child-rearing partner.

2. List a few family members, friends or close neighbors who would make good partners. This may take some thought.

3. Ask your "first choice" if he or she is willing to partner with you.

4. Define your roles and decide who will make key decisions.

For example, who will be responsible for the following? (*This list is intended only as a starting point.*)

	Me	Partner	Together
Doctor and dentist appointments			
Choose school			
Buy clothes			
Manage extracurricular activities			
Find and manage child care			

Grocery shopping			
Pay bills			
Dry cleaners			
Clean house (divide chores)			
Bathe the kids			
Read bedtime stories			
Feed pets			
Lawn care			

5. Periodically discuss how the partnership is going. Don't put it on "cruise control"—actively manage the relationship. Fill out the following:

We will meet every _____ months to talk about our expectations for each other, our happiness with the balance of workload and how we think the kids are doing. The first meeting is scheduled for - _____.

6. Celebrate the successes of the partnership! Schedule a fun night out, dinner or some other opportunity to get together every few months and celebrate how well your kids are doing thanks to your great parenting partnership.

Sanity Savers

- Don't try to do it all alone—we all need partners in this business of raising great kids.

- Create a strong child-rearing partnership.

- Remember that our child-rearing partnerships are as individualized as we are. Consider what works best for your kids, you and your partner

- Schedule time monthly to talk to your childrearing partner about the kids.

- Realize that if you are divorced you will have to work even harder to communicate.

STEP FIVE

Building Your Support Network
It Takes a Village

Because of my travel schedule, Dan and I rarely had a chance to go out during the week, but one week I happened to be in town and a friend gave us tickets to an Avalanche hockey game. Of course, it was a busy night—Holden had hockey practice and Regan had gymnastics—and my mom was out of town and the caregiver was sick. My hopes for a fun evening out with my husband were fading.

I ran several scenarios through my head, trying to figure out how we could pull this off, and was about to give up when I realized that there were people out there who would be more than happy to help us. I called a friend who had offered to help on several occasions and she agreed to take Regan to gymnastics, and my sister was all too happy to take Holden to hockey practice—she loves spending time with the kids. So Dan and I got a much-needed night out.

It wasn't always this hectic in our household, but with four active family members, getting us all where we needed to be on time was sometimes like performing a magic act. At least once a week we got caught in scheduling gridlock.

We all need to build a support network, and if you don't have a primary partner, building that network is even more important. Your support network is the "village" of family members, friends and neighbors you can rely on when the unexpected happens, when schedules collide and you can't be everywhere at once. With kids, the unexpected tends to happen a lot, and for working moms, keeping schedules straight can a bit like building a house of cards.

The kind souls in your support network will be your lifesavers, and you'll need them more often than you might imagine. In our family, there were days that were literally a series of unfortunate events. One day, all within a few hours, my flight was delayed, the kids both got sick, Dan had a meeting he couldn't miss and the caregiver quit with no notice. Gretchen to village: SOS!

Asking for Help

Asking for help is hard to do. The working moms I interviewed at Warren Village agreed that this is one of their biggest challenges. They said that needing help feels like a weakness or a shortcoming. *I should be able to do this myself. If I were a better mom, I could figure this out. Other moms can do it—why can't I?*

Sharon Knight, Warren Village executive director, says, "I was pretty cautious about asking other people to help unless there was something that I could do for them. So instead of just asking for favors, it was more like bartering. I felt guilty asking for help if I couldn't provide something in return, and I know a lot of women who live in the village feel that way too."

Rachel Contizano, formerly of Warren Village, says building a support network has been hard for her. "I hate to say that to this day my mom is still the only support system I have. I ask her to help with any and all emergencies with my son. I've always had a hard time asking others for help, and unfortunately, I don't really know a lot of people I think I can rely on.

"A lot of women are embarrassed to ask for help or believe that they shouldn't ask for help. I was taught not to ask for help, to do things on my own and that you're weak if you ask for help. In order to overcome that, I had to start with little things, like asking a friend to watch my son for a couple hours. I didn't want to put the burden on anyone.

"I think, too, that there are so many bad stereotypes out there that you're lazy. So when you have to ask for help, you're not treated very well by society or even by the organizations or agencies that are set up to help. So it can be burdensome."

We all need to get over this belief that asking for help is a sign of weakness. Everyone needs help. And most people like to help.

Set Up Your Network before You Need Help

Whether you like it or not, there are going to be times when you need help. Accepting this reality is the first building block for your village.

This step has been relatively easy for me because my mom, sister, godmom and sister-in-law all live in my city, but I have many friends who don't have family in town who have also built a support network, and you can, too. Think of this as having a Plan A, a Plan B and Plans C, D and E! It takes a little time to pull your safety net together, but once it's in place, you'll have less stress because you'll know you have backup plans in place.

You'll also have less guilt because fewer important tasks will fall through the cracks. "I can still remember how panicked I felt the day my son called to say he had to be at school in twenty minutes for a concert rehearsal and there was no way I could get him there in time," Sharon Knight says. "I had the concert in my calendar, but I didn't know they were doing a full rehearsal before the concert, and that meant getting there an hour sooner than I planned. I started calling everyone I could think of and finally found a neighbor who could drive him to school on time. I didn't have a formal agreement with this neighbor, but she and her husband were both retired and said they missed all the activities and liked seeing Jacob, so they said they'd be delighted to help at any time. And it wasn't 'tit for tat,' but since they didn't really like to cook anymore, I made meals for them whenever I could."

Sharon says that what she learned from the experience was the importance of not only having a network of people who could help but also having all their numbers readily available on speed-dial. "I asked everyone on my list, 'If I need your help, what's the fastest way to get ahold of you?'"

When Jeanne Saunders' children were babies, she was part of a baby-sitting co-op in her neighborhood. "There were at least twenty-five moms in the co-op and we all pitched in to help take care of each other's kids," she says. "Someone kept track of the hours, and I'll tell you what—it saved my bacon many times! It also gave the kids a broader perspective because they got to see how other families functioned and that I wasn't the only mom who worked."

To begin setting up your network, make a list of the neighbors, family members and friends who would be happy to help you and your kids when Plans A and B collapse. There might be other moms in your neighborhood who are looking for support, too, and you can all help each other. You might have a neighbor who is retired and would love your kids to go to her house for an hour after school until you can pick them up or would be willing to take care of them when you have an emergency and no time to call in someone who lives farther away. You might have friends who would feel honored to be part of your village and enjoy the chance to help out and spend time with your kids.

You're raising great kids, so of course your family and friends will want to get to know them better. And because you have great friends and family members, your kids will benefit from spending time with them. It's a win-win! My kids have strong relationships with my family members and friends and have benefited greatly from having each of them in their lives.

Years back, at the beginning of a school year, a friend told me she and her husband didn't have any vacation days to cover their kids' sick days for the next two months. "Would it be okay if our kids came over to your house if they get sick and can't go to school?" she asked. We worked out an arrangement with my caregiver, but my friend never had to use it. The important part was that she had a fallback plan in place and the peace of mind that goes with it. You can never have too many plans!

"My sister-in-law has a modified work schedule and is an amazing support, and friends and family are helpful, too," Jody Camp says. She's also been fortunate to have had bosses who were supportive and understanding about working and raising kids. "Having a supportive boss is key for me. All of my female bosses (and one male!) leave when their kids have emergencies, so I feel comfortable doing the same." Jody has family and friends she can call on if the kids are sick or there's an emergency, but "I want to be there for the emergencies," she says, "so I leave work to handle them and my husband and I share the responsibility of leaving work if our kids get sick."

The key is to set up your network so that it covers the things you can't or don't need to do yourself. Your support network can include professional services such as temporary caregivers, friends, family and neighbors. There's a service in Denver that will send out a temporary caregiver on an hour's notice if your child is sick. I have also used www.care.com to hire my after-school caregivers, and most agencies do the background checks for you. While some parents balk at the idea of having strangers take care of their kids, the variety of people my kids met and interacted with outside our circle of family and friends definitely benefited them by widening their horizons.

My friends developed their support networks in a wide variety of ways. Shannon Oury moved to a small town with relatives who were available to help out. Susan Walters developed a strong relationship with a caregiver who then became a member of her support network, volunteering for "emergency watch duty" and weekend child care at no cost. Lisa Walker has used her parents and neighbors as an extended network of support.

As Deidre Bacala says, "You must have people 'on call' around you. Add them to your approved day-care pickup list. Complete medical authorizations 'just in case.' Don't be afraid to ask for help! If the shoe was on the other foot, you would want to help out."

This is great advice. My sister Pam and the kids' godmom, Annie, were on the approved pickup list and had notarized paperwork on medical-decision authority.

Learning Who and How to Trust

An important factor that can be a hurdle for many working moms is learning to trust people outside our circle of family and friends to take care of our kids. Of course, we want to be cautious about who watches our kids, especially when they're too young to articulate if someone is harming them or ignoring their needs, but we can't build a strong support network if we don't learn how to trust people. For some moms, the issue of trust comes up right after they give birth and realize that they don't even trust the baby's father at first. Some new moms trust only their own moms or aunts to help. Having initial fear or even trepidation about placing your child in someone else's hands is understandable and normal, but working moms have to work through these fears for the sake of our kids and our own sanity.

I have a single-dad friend who is "mom" to his son, and this has been a huge struggle for him. During the first year I knew him, he had one "approved" teenage baby-sitter for evenings out, no family in town at all, and no backup plan in the event that his son got sick and couldn't go to school other than calling in sick to work himself. After the eighth day that this happened, and as his one baby-sitter was headed off to college, he realized he needed other resources and might need to start to trust other people.

Building Trust in Your Network

Here are some tips to help you overcome a lack of trust in building your network:

- If you're using a professional service or agency, be sure it does thorough background checks and rated the performance of its employees.

- Let your service providers know that you'll be dropping in periodically to see how things are going.

- If using a caregiver cam is the assurance you need, do it.

- Frequently ask your kids to tell you about their time with the service provider. Ask them specific questions about what they did, what they had for lunch, how they had fun and other questions that encourage them to talk about their experience.

Tips for Maintaining a 'Happy Village'

A happy village is a healthy village! Here are some suggestions for maintaining great relationships with these wonderful people in your life:

Communicate Frequently and Face-to-Face

It's important to spend time with your village members so they know that you value them as individuals in addition to appreciating their help and support with your kids. Regularly ask them how it's going, if they feel burdened, if there's anything about their roles that they'd like to change—they'll appreciate it. As your kids get older and change, your needs will change and the lives of your support network will change, so you'll need to stay open to the need to make adjustments.

I met with my mom at the beginning of each new school year and the kids' summer break to ask her about her ability to cover during sick days, how much time she wanted to spend with the kids, if there were days or dates she wasn't available and other logistics. Even though my mom loved being with her grandkids and helping to take care of them, she had an active life of her own, and it wouldn't have been fair for me to assume that she would always be at our beck and call.

Show Your Gratitude

No matter how available the people in our networks may appear to be, we must never forget that they are helping us out of the goodness of their hearts. They are the most valuable volunteers in our world, and we must never make assumptions about their time or take them for granted in any way. They are not hired help.

And they may not be comfortable saying "no" to you. Take them out for coffee. Thank them for their help and bring them a small gift. The time they spend helping you is a precious gift. Ask them if the arrangement you have with them is still working for them and if there's anything they'd like to adjust or stop doing.

Encourage Their Freedom to Say "No"

A very important ingredient in having a strong support team is for each person to feel comfortable saying no. That's why it's great to have a network with a lot of people in it. If your villages know that they aren't your last resort, that you still have Plans D and E to put into action, they'll feel OK about saying no. With that worry out of the way, they'll also feel great when they can say yes.

When my mom was helping with the kids, I made her assure me she would always tell me if she couldn't watch them or didn't feel up to it. The caregiver service was my twenty-four-hour-a-day last-minute backup, so Mom could say no at the last minute and it didn't create a problem for me or the kids.

Treat Your Support Network with Respect

Whatever you do, don't take your network for granted! Even if you know your Aunt Betty loves the kids and is happy to jump in at the last moment, making this a habit will eventually dampen Aunt Betty's enthusiasm to help you, no matter how much she enjoys her nieces and nephews. Make it a habit to reach out to your network as soon as you suspect you're going to need help. That way you can line up Plans C and D ahead of time and cancel your request if it turns out you or your primary child-rearing partner can handle it.

Another important aspect of treating your network with respect is keeping your word about how much time you need them or how often. To me, this seems obvious, so I'm always amazed when I see someone abusing his or her support network and taking the gift of having a village for granted. If you tell your baby-sitter you'll be home by 9 p.m., you need to be home by 9 p.m. or you're going to lose a member of your village!

Summary

Building a support network that helps you develop multiple game plans is an important step in reducing stress in your life and the lives of your kids. I've seen many of my friends do this in an ad-hoc way, but what

I'm proposing is a deliberate strategy that's well-thought-out and proactive rather than seat-of-the-pants and reactive. Start by thinking through who can be in this network and take the steps outlined in this chapter to set expectations and communicate with each person. The result will be the assurance that no matter what happens (mostly!), you'll have a game plan in place.

'I'm a Great Working Mom' Exercises

1. Times when I'm going to need help:

_____

_____

_____

_____

_____

_____

_____

2. Current resources I can utilize:

Person and/or company	For what help	To do's (talk to them, etc.)

3. New resources I need to find:

Person and/or company	For what help	To do's (talk to them, etc.)

4. Ways I can build my trust in these resources:

_____

_____

_____

_____

_____

Sanity Savers

- Be willing to ask for help.

- Know who you can ask for help ahead of time!

- Create a support network of family members, friends and neighbors who you can rely on when the unexpected happens.

- Set up your network so that it covers the things you can't or don't need to do yourself. Our support network can also include professional services.

- Learn to trust the right people outside your circle of family and friends to take care of your kids.

STEP SIX

Finding the Right Child Care
Another 'Partner' in Your Life

One day our receptionist at the Women's Foundation was madly looking for Susan Walters, who worked for me. "Her son Corey just called and thinks he broke his ankle," she said.

My response: "I think I might be interested in this as well. Corey is my summer caregiver and today's his first day!" Fortunately, it turned out that Corey had only a bad sprain from jumping on our trampoline.

Even though things don't always go smoothly with childcare, this is one of the most important aspects of being a great working mom. We can't possibly do our best at work if we're worrying about whether our kids are safe and being well-cared for in a healthy environment. We all need to know that our kids are in good hands. I am not a child-care expert, I'm a great mom who has some experience in child care, and this chapter is intended as an overview of things to think about that may reduce your stress.

Notice that I didn't title this chapter the perfect child care. There is no perfect child-care solution. No one is going to do things *exactly* like you do. No one can fill your shoes. Even our own moms aren't going to raise our kids exactly as we will, so for some moms, finding good-quality child care begins with letting go of the notion that the people who care for our kids have to do it the way we would do it. As Lora Ledermann put it, "You'll never find another 'you,' so stop trying to find that person."

My kids had after-school caregivers who could cook dinner and those who couldn't do mac and cheese without burning it, caregivers who could help with algebra and those who could hardly add up the hours they worked. Caregivers run the gamut, and finding the right one for you is critical for your sanity.

"Having a safe, healthy and educational environment, near my work, for my kids means everything to me," Jody Camp says. "I don't stress, because I know their friends and teachers are doing a lot more for them than I could alone. My kids thrived in day care."

Start Looking Early

Having the right child care allows you to go off to work each day knowing that your child is receiving good-quality care from a loving person, allowing you to be productive and focused at work. Don't put this important decision off until the last minute. Nothing about finding the right child care is easy, and it takes time to find what you need, so don't put off your search.

Sharon Knight says that when her son was young, she looked at about thirty-five day-care places before she found one she felt comfortable with. "Finding competent caregivers that will help our kids to thrive is difficult but incredibly important," she says. "If I didn't know the setting and the professionals were appropriate, I wouldn't have been as successful in my job."

Learn as much as you can about your options early in your pregnancy. About four months before our first child was born, we started asking our friends and friends of friends about their child care, why they chose it and how it was working out for them. We talked with people who used caregivers, au pairs, in-house child care and day-care centers. It turned out that one of my mom's friends had a daughter whose caregiver was from Guatemala and would be looking for a new family soon because the little boy was beginning first grade in the fall. The mom told me that in four years, the caregiver had never missed a day of work. Spanish was her first language, which was great because we wanted our kids to be bilingual, and she was a very loving person. She sounded like a great fit, but we couldn't afford her.

After thinking about this hurdle for a while, I remembered that we had friends who were expecting a baby the same month we were. We approached them about sharing the caregiver to cut the cost for both of us, and they agreed. The caregiver was happy with this arrangement, and it made her affordable for two families. She was a wonderful, loving caregiver, and I knew our kids were safe and happy with her. I think that when they were very young, they thought they had two moms, one who spoke English and one who spoke Spanish!

Having More Than One Great Mom Is OK

Which brings up another important point: If the idea of your kids bonding with other caregivers makes you feel insecure, keep in mind that kids who can bond with more than one person are healthy and well-adjusted. Rather than taking away from your relationship with them, it will make it stronger. The more people who love and care about your kids, the better off they'll be. And as your kids get older, they'll respect you for fostering these strong relationships in their lives.

When we hold our newborns for the first time, it can feel like we're the only people in the world, like the sun and the moon revolve around us. But in truth, we need an entire village to raise great kids, and our child-care providers play some of the most important parts in our kids' lives and our lives. Having strong relationships with these important villagers will make things easier for everyone in the family. No one is ever going to replace you as your kids' mom, assuming that you're the caring, loving, responsible human being you must be to be reading this book! You're a great mom and always will be.

Child-Care Priorities

There are many factors to keep in mind when you interview child-care providers or visit child-care centers. The following seven are important for many parents, but since our needs are as individual as our kids, add your own factors to this list before you begin your search:

➤ Safety and security of the kids
➤ Location
➤ Hours of operation or availability
➤ Ratio of child-care providers to kids
➤ Credentials, training and licensing
➤ Curriculum
➤ Recommendations from other parents

Safety is the most important factor. "You always want to do your research about any child care—online reviews, asking other parents, visiting the child-care center and, of course, asking a lot of questions," Rachel Contizano says.

"The most important things I looked at were location, hours of operation, safety and quality. This way I knew my son was in a good learning environment while I was at work or looking for work."

Whether you enroll your child in a center or hire a baby-sitter or caregiver, be sure you have the freedom to occasionally drop in for a quick visit. If there are a lot of restrictions about when parents can drop in, this may be a red flag. If your child has special needs, is food-sensitive or has allergies, you'll need to be sure the center or provider understands the seriousness of these conditions and has a plan in place to handle them appropriately.

Once you've completed your list of factors and criteria, arrange them in order from most important to least important. You may not be able to find a center or a child-care provider who meets every one of your criteria, but by focusing on your highest priorities, you can make sure you find what's most important to you. In our case, we wanted someone dependable and loving who had a lot of experience with babies, we needed someone we could afford and we wanted someone whose first language was Spanish, but we were willing to give in on that preference.

Clear Communication Is Key

Communication with caregivers is critical. When you enroll your child in a child-care center or program or hire a caregiver or baby-sitter, put your expectations in writing. If you're using a day-care center, make sure you're clear about what the care providers will and won't do, how your child will be spending his or her time every day and how emergencies will be handled.

If you're hiring a child-care provider to take care of your kids at home, in addition to writing down your expectations, you'll also want to document your commitments to them, such as pay, vacations, benefits and sick time. Make sure you review this document with the person you hire and answer any questions they may have. This will ensure that your relationship gets off on the right foot and lets the child-care provider know exactly what you're looking for and what he or she can expect.

While having expectations and commitments in writing creates a great foundation, for the relationship to work well, you need to have open and ongoing communication. It's very difficult to have open discussion when you're dropping off or picking up your child, so you must schedule time to meet with the child-care provider when someone else can take care of your kids so the two of you can have an uninterrupted adult conversation. Some moms like to meet with the child-care provider or day-care teacher every couple of months or as needed, while other moms feel the need for fewer formal meetings but more e-mail or text communication.

We scheduled time to sit down with our caregivers and have a conversation about how things were going twice a year. My mom watched the kids so Dan, the caregiver and I could all speak freely and without interruption. We covered questions and subjects such as:

➢ What can we do to help you?

➢ Are you happy with the relationship you have with our child?

➢ Are you happy with the relationship you have with us?

➢ What concerns do you have about our child?

➢ Upcoming challenges—weaning them of a bottle, potty training, etc.—and how we would team up on strategy.

➢ Child-care needs for the next few months—any changes in needs, hours, etc.

➢ Upcoming vacations.

It's also good to ask child-care providers if there's something they'd like to share that you haven't asked them about. This ensures that they have an opportunity to express anything they think you need to know.

Easing the Transition

Before your children are on their own with the child-care provider or at the day-care center, spend a little time with them to ease the transition. This is easy to do at home and helps your children and the child-care provider to get to know each other with your support. Many day-care centers permit parents to stay for the first hour of the day during the first week of day care or have other ways for parents to help their kids to make a successful transition.

When it's time for you to leave, don't sneak out or your children may feel abandoned or scared. Even if they're having fun and don't notice you leaving, at some point they'll look for you. Say good-bye cheerfully, tell them that you know they will have a great day and that you can't wait to hear about it when you pick them up. When you pick them up, don't ask them if they missed you or dwell on how much you missed them. Of course you missed each other, but keep your focus on the positive parts of your day. Share something fun or funny that happened during your day and ask your children to do the same. If you constantly tell them you missed them or ask if they missed you, they'll think they should miss you and you'll be reinforcing the negative instead of the positive. Instead, try saying, "What wonderful things did you do today? Tell me all about them."

One of my friends who has a stepson took turns with his mom dropping him off at day care in the morning. When his mom dropped him off, she told him she'd miss him and sometimes even shed a few tears. He often clung to her neck and cried, and many times the day-care teacher would have to pry him from his mom's arms and settle his tantrum. When his stepmom dropped him off, she was positive and sounded excited about his day. On these days, he typically skipped into the playroom and eagerly greeted his friends. Kids will often feel what we're feeling and mirror our actions and emotions, so if you want your kids to have easier transitions, you have to handle your own issues first.

Surviving the Clingy Phase

Taking a positive approach will go a long way, but most kids go through phases where they're clingier and have a harder time with your leaving. Most of the time when I left for the airport, my kids waved good-bye to me without any fuss as I left. Regan came up with the phrase "Don't 'formiss' me"—her combination of forget and miss—to say as she smiled and waved good-bye to me. But each of my kids went through a period of about two months during which the caregiver had to practically peel them off of me as they sobbed. I remember driving to the airport with tears streaming down my face, feeling like the worst mom in the world.

If your child starts having a more difficult time with your leaving or dropping them off, sit down with your child-care provider and talk about it. Maybe something has changed or your child-care provider is going through a difficult personal time and the kids are picking up on it. Maybe your child is just going through a phase like mine did. (By the way, neither of my kids remembers this phase!) If your kids are old enough, talk to them about it, too. When one of my co-worker's daughters suddenly didn't want to go to school and didn't want her parents to go to work, it turned out that she'd seen a movie clip about an earthquake and she was terrified that if she and her parents split up, they could be separated forever. It took some time for her parents to ease her mind, but if they hadn't asked her, they may never have known what was causing her fear and anxiety.

Streamlining Communication

If you want caregivers to keep you informed about what's happening on a daily basis, make it easy and convenient for them to do so. Have a place where they can write down important information during the day, such as when the baby had bottles, how much and when and if the baby napped, what the kids had for snack, did they do their homework (or not!). At the end of the day, you'll be excited to see your child, and he or she will be very excited to see you, too, so having a conversation with the child-care provider right then will be almost impossible.

If you have child care in your home, consider making a daily communication sheet to make the process easier and more efficient. We used our "sanity bible" (to be discussed in Step Seven) so that all our information was in the same place. These sheets allowed me to catch up on what had been going on while I was gone for two or three days at a time and helped me develop a level of comfort level with the child care my kids were receiving. Most day-care centers will provide this type of information to you on a daily or weekly basis.

If you're a working mom who embraces technology, you may want your child-care provider to record information on an iPad or to text you updates and questions throughout the day. What's important is for you and your child-care provider to come up with a system to keep the lines of communication open at all times.

Changing Child-Care Needs

Your priorities for child care will change over time, and you need to reevaluate your needs periodically. Our first caregiver couldn't drive, which was no problem when the kids were young, because the park was a block away and they didn't need to be driven too many places, but as they became older, having someone who could drive them to activities was more important. As your kids grow older, you may also need to find new caretakers who are more attuned to whatever ages they are. A great caregiver for an infant isn't always a great caregiver for a toddler or older kids. Your kids may transition from day-care centers to after-school care to being mostly on their own, with someone to check on them periodically. Finding the right solution is a very personal thing and changes over time.

For Susan Walters, moving around the country as her kids were growing up meant finding child care over and over again. "Moving a lot and changing child care is hard on the kids," she says, "but I always tried to make sure the kids understood that a) I would make the best choices possible and correct any mistakes as soon as I was able and b) bad day-care leaders and teachers are a part of life, just like bad teachers and bosses would be later in life. Sometimes you just have to deal with it even if it sucks. It wasn't just a lesson for me—it was important for the kids to learn that, too."

Susan was fortunate to eventually find a baby-sitter who became like a member of the family. "We found her quite by accident. We got in a desperate place and had a last-chance day-care thing going on and Jinny happened to be working there. Jinny took to the kids and they took to her and she stayed in their lives for years. I was able to call on her not just for emergency child care but emergency transportation, too. And she used to volunteer to take the kids overnight or for a weekend, no charge."

When Susan's daughter Lindsay was injured falling out of a shopping cart and they had to ride in an ambulance to a hospital more than seventy miles away, Jinny drove three hours to pick up Susan's car and drive it to the hospital so they could go home.

My care needs changed early on in motherhood. When Holden was thirteen months old and my delivery date for Regan was two weeks away, I was sitting at my office desk thinking, "Wouldn't it be nice if Holden had a place he could go for a few hours every week to socialize with other kids?" Our caregiver couldn't drive and I had no friends with kids and practically no friends in Denver at all given my weekly travel schedule. So I pulled out the phone book (we still had phone books back then) and started by calling the Montessori schools because I had attended a Montessori preschool. The first two I called were a bust—they took kids only full time—but the third had a program where kids from eighteen months to three years old could attend for two and a half hours a day a few days a week or all five days, and it was located just twenty blocks from our house and ten blocks from my office. They had an opening for a boy (classes were equal-gender) in the fall, when Holden would just be eighteen months old. Eureka!

I later found out that this preschool is *impossible* to get into and that many of my friends were on a waiting list and never got their kids in. Needless to say, they were incredibly annoyed that I'd found it in the phone book and hadn't even known I was applying to one of the best preschools in Denver. Regan and Holden both attended that preschool until they were three, and my mom did the driving back and forth. It gave my mom quality time with the kids, and they loved the school.

Advocating for Child-Care Help

"I think that any mom would do her very best and allocate as much of the budget as possible for quality day care," Sharon Knight says. "Some might actually go over what they would think is a realistic budget amount because making sure their kids are in good hands is the most important decision in their life."

When Sharon's son was young, she looked at thirty-five child-care centers before she found one she felt comfortable with. "Finding competent caregivers that will not only keep our kids safe but help them to thrive, though difficult, is incredibly important," she says. "If I didn't trust that the setting and professionals were appropriate, I just wouldn't have been able to do my job well."

Women who don't have the financial means to pay for good-quality child care often have to be strong advocates for themselves in order to get their kids what they need. Many of the women I interviewed have struggled to find quality child care that's affordable and meets their needs. One woman had to quit her job because she couldn't find child care at 6 a.m. when she needed to be at work. One of the greatest challenges single women face is finding good-quality child care that they can afford.

Rachel Contizano says that when she and her son moved to Colorado, it was extremely difficult for her to find affordable care. Colorado has some of the highest child-care costs in the country, and the only way Rachel could obtain care for her son was to apply for Temporary Assistance for Needy Families (TANF). "They only have so much money to give, so they turned me down at first. I talked to the manager to get help and it was a headache, but they eventually covered three days a week. I had to pay for the other two days. We have to be willing to advocate for what our kids need."

Rachel encourages all women to dig deep and find the courage to go to bat for their kids. "If something's going on with your child at school, you're going to go down to the school and you're going to talk to them. That's advocating for your child. And that's the same type of thing you do when you're trying to get services. You go to them and you fight. You look at the policies, you do your homework and you don't take no for an answer if the policies are in place to help you."

She acknowledges that the fight can be exhausting, but she's committed to doing the best she can. "Don't let anybody say no to something that's possible. When I only got three days of child care covered, I didn't have the energy to fight anymore. But eight months later, I picked the fight back up and I got what I needed."

Summary

No matter what financial resources you have, placing the care of your child in the hands of others is probably one of the hardest things you'll do as a working mom. Just remember that you're a great mom and you're providing the best child-care solution for you, given the resources you have at hand.

'I'm a Great Working Mom' Exercises

1. What is my ideal child-care schedule?

Days: _____

Times: _____

2. What are my priorities regarding child care?

    1. _____

    2. _____

    3. _____

    4. _____

    5. _____

3. What can I afford to pay for child care:

    $_____/week

4. What options do I have for childcare services?

    - Caregiver services:_____

    - In-home providers:_____

    - Day-care centers:_____

5. Who can I talk to about their own kids' child care?

    _____
    _____
    _____
    _____
    _____
    _____
    _____

Questions for prospective providers:

Are they certified and have they passed a background check?

Can I talk to at least three references?

Do they have experience with kids the same age as mine?

Why do they want to do child care?

Do they know infant/toddler/child CPR and emergency care?

What would they do in an emergency?

What do they like doing most with kids?

What would their favorite day look like?

What are their expectations for pay? Benefits such as paid vacation, health care and mileage?

How long do they expect to work in child care?

Can I observe them with other kids they watch?

If it's a center, what does a typical day look like?

What is the caregiver/child ratio?

Do they provide snacks?

Is there a place for me to store diapers, bottles, etc., or do I have to bring them every day?

What is the facility's average tenure for caregivers? What is its turnover rate?

Can I talk to two other parents?

Can I bring my child when he/she is sick?

Sanity Savers

- Prioritize your child-care requirements.

- Keep an open mind and trust your gut.

- Don't put off the search—it takes time to find what we need.

- Remember that kids who can bond with more than one person are healthy and well-adjusted.

- Put expectations and commitments in writing

- If your child starts having a difficult time with your leaving or dropping him or her off, talk about it with your child-care provider.

- If you want your caregiver to keep you informed on a daily basis, make it easy and convenient for him or her to do so.

STEP SEVEN

Becoming Organized
A Key Ingredient of Sanity!

Picture this. I'm on my way out the door with my kids to drop them off at my mom's on the way to work because our caregiver is on vacation. We can't find Regan's favorite shoes and she's in tears. We can't find Holden's favorite toy and *he's* in tears. I can't find the scarf that matches my outfit and *I'm* nearly in tears!

It's one thing to be a bit disorganized before we have kids, and it's something else entirely after we introduce kids into the mix. Before I had kids, spontaneity and disorganization were a part of life. After I had kids, it meant somebody couldn't find their other shoe and I was about to be late for a meeting. Being organized at home and at work can do a lot to ease the stress of being a great mom. If you're the spontaneous type and it doesn't bother you when you can't find something, don't be surprised if raising kids changes that. If it doesn't, more power to you!

I'm lucky in that organization comes fairly easily to me, but when my kids were born, I realized I had to take my organizing skills to a whole new level. Before they were born, I could jot down a few dinner ideas, head to the grocery store and return with the makings of a few days' worth of meals. Not much time or thought went into it, and it was no big deal. After I had kids, I spent my Sundays making meals for the entire week, and my menu planning and shopping list had to be highly organized. If

I forgot an ingredient, I couldn't very well leave the pots on the stove and the kids to their own devices while I dashed out to the store.

You can pay a price for lack of organization. When the kids were attending the Montessori School of Denver, parents had to volunteer for twenty hours each school year or pay $250 instead. My travel schedule made volunteering in the classroom nearly impossible (and I must admit I'm not a "three-year-old" kind of person), but I found out that if we kept a class pet for the summer, we would get credit for all my volunteer hours for the entire year. Perfect—I could do this! But, of course, my schedule became busy and I forgot to make a note on my calendar to reserve one of the pets. By the time I approached Holden's teacher about it, the only pet left was a five-foot corn snake named Slither. Now, my ex-husband hates snakes, *really* hates them, and you can imagine the conversation that ensued about our keeping a live snake for the entire summer! The punishment for being disorganized.

Not everyone finds organization easy, but no matter how natural or challenging it is for you, there are tips that can make it easier. By organizing your time and your space, you'll have more time for yourself and your kids, you'll have less stress and you won't waste time trying to figure out when the next doctor's appointment is or what time your kid's Little League game starts. In other words, being organized will help you to be a great mom.

Plan Further Ahead

Once your first child is born, your days of throwing a bag into the car and taking off for a long weekend at the last minute are probably over. Overnight you go from wearing a shoulder bag to wearing a baby and carrying a diaper bag. As your child grows older, the diaper bag will be replaced by a hockey bag or a dance bag, and eventually your kids will be old enough to tote their own stuff around. And someday your kids will keep their own schedules and you can go back to the simple days of keeping just one calendar straight—your own. But for now, to stay sane, you're going to want to plan further ahead.

Start with your weekly and monthly schedules. When my kids were young in the late '90s, technology wasn't what it is today, and our family kept a one-page 8 ½-by-11 spreadsheet for each week and manually wrote *everything* on it so that each sheet had all the information for a week. And we clipped several of these spreadsheets together so that we could see what was coming up for the next three to four months. For each day of the week, we tracked everything—what city Mom is in and when she's leaving, who's taking the kids to school, who's picking them up, who has ballet, who has a birthday party. I also incorporated the kids' chores into the schedule as they got older.

I called this master schedule our "sanity bible." It made us feel secure to know that, at a glance, we could remind ourselves of everything we needed to do. With our kids in ballet, soccer, ice hockey, lacrosse, piano lessons, etc., things could become very confusing very quickly. We always kept our sanity bible in the same place on the kitchen desk so that we always knew where it was and could refer to it easily. Anyone who moved it was in big trouble!

When the kids were in middle school and things started to get even crazier, we augmented the sanity bible with a dry-erase month-at-a-glance calendar on the refrigerator, with color-coding by person. This let us see the month's schedule at a glance as we raced out the door and was a visual reminder of what chores were assigned to each of us for the week. (Isn't it great when the kids are old enough to pick up the dog poop?) I also tried to review the weekly calendar with the kids every Sunday night so that we had a "battle plan" for the week.

When the kids were in high school and Dan and I divorced, we started using our Outlook calendars to "invite" each other and our kids to activities, including sports practices and parent-teacher meetings, and to post our travel schedules, school holidays and important dates like back-to-school night. This made it much easier for us to keep track of everything. Even today Dan and I have a rule that whenever either of us puts something on our calendar that involves our kids, we invite each other to the event. All of this has also taught my kids how to manage their own calendars.

Tips from Other Great Working Moms

Of all the tips offered by the moms interviewed for this book, creating a master calendar was by far the most-mentioned. "A master calendar is a key to sanity and organization," as Margaret Kelly says. "It takes a little time at first, but it's worth it. I would put all of the kids' school commitments on the calendar and then book my work travel around that as best I could. I constantly have a to-do list because trying to remember everything doesn't work. When I'm getting ready in the morning, I have a piece of paper on the counter and I write down whatever tasks or events come to mind and then I immediately put them all on the master list. You can keep your master list in the note section on your iPhone and e-mail to yourself, so it's really easy. I categorize the list by work, home and personal, so everything's easy to see. The minute I write it down, it's out of my brain. So it makes room, if you will."

Shannon Oury used a big calendar with dry-erase markers. Everyone in the family had a different color. "For years, I was constantly coordinating," she says. "Where did each kid need to be at what time and who got assigned to that? And who got assigned to the dentist and who got assigned for pickup and drop-off. I have a really great partner as a husband, but I was always in charge of air traffic control. I was unwilling to relinquish control of the assurance that we had everything covered."

Jody Camp has a master calendar for the kids, and she and her husband also each have busy work calendars, so they always have a lot to fit into any given day. "We have both calendars taped next to each other right there in the kitchen," she says. "And it's not just a month, it's three months. So we do thirty-, sixty- and ninety-day planning. I've put all of my business skills into managing my family."

Involve Your Kids in Schedule Planning

When your kids are old enough, get them involved in the scheduling, too. When my kids were young, I heard a judge on the Colorado Supreme Court give a presentation, and something she said left a lasting impression. Rebecca Love Kourlis, who was also my neighbor and friend, advised that we all ask our kids which events are the most important to them so we can make those events a priority. We can't attend everything, and talking to our kids about this lets them know that they're important to us and that we'll do our best to make it to the most important events. Margaret Kelly also suggests that we "sit down with our kids when we know we can't be at an event and explain why and point out all the events we can attend." I've found this to be really helpful because sometimes what I assume is important to the kids really isn't. Remember that band concert in Chapter 1?!

Time-Saving Tips from Organized Moms

Here are some other great tips from the great moms I spoke with:

"Definitely a master calendar (Google calendar is my best friend). And Sunday weekly menu planning based on the weekly events. Easy meals for soccer-practice nights and meals made with the help of the kids on other nights."

—Lora Ledermann

"After having missed an event for my oldest when she was in second grade, I realized I needed to do something to coordinate all activities. That's when my husband (always a tech guy) showed me Microsoft Outlook. "Today at a Glance" was how I started each day. It truly saved my sanity!"

—Gloria Bokenkamp

"We use a calendar and a dry-erase board. After dinner, I write the jobs we're each supposed to do the next day and the time frame we have to do them in. When we complete a job, we initial it. My daughter can see what she needs to do the next day when she gets home from school."

—Ruby

"A master calendar was essential. I also kept extra things in the car (snacks, water, change, clothes) that my son might need and forget to tell me about until the last second. As silly as it might sound, I also sent myself reminders and posted notes in various places—helped me stay on track when unexpected challenges often disrupted my planned schedule."

—Sharon Knight

"Prepare the night before! Mornings are hectic enough trying to get everyone ready and fed (including myself!). Whether it's swim lessons, splash day, show and tell, etc.—set everything out the night before. Lifesaving and sanity-saving! We also keep all the kid shoes in one spot all the time—no panic in the mornings looking for them."

—Deidre Bacala

White Space in the Schedule Equals Sanity

Rachel Contizano not only keeps a master calendar, but she also works hard to make sure the schedule isn't overly full. With our busy lives, keeping white space on our calendars can be a challenge, but it's an important part of keeping stress at a manageable level. Overscheduling your life and your kids' lives will only increase that stress. We all sigh with relief when we have an evening when nobody has to be anywhere or do anything, and those free evenings can be some of the best times we have as a family. Set a goal to have one or two evenings with *nothing* on the calendar—the free time will really help empower you to be a great mom.

A Place for Everything and Everything in Its Place

A key component of staying organized is having a designated place for everything. Period. This requires some potentially uncomfortable discipline at first, but it will make your life much easier. If you're not in the habit of keeping items in the same place all the time, you may need to use Post-it notes or some other form of labeling until everyone in your family knows where everything belongs. Have an assigned place for your bills, other important mail, your keys, tickets to events, your master calendar and everything else. Giving everything its own "home" is essential, and it's possible only if you don't have more things than you have space for. If you always have a laundry basket or two filled with clothes that you don't put away because they won't fit in your dresser or closet, do yourself a favor and give away enough clothes so that the ones you keep will fit in the space you have.

Jody Camp has taken this concept to a new level. Not only does everything in her home have a place, but her family also has a system for making sure everyone has what they need for activities. They gather all the kids' stuff for the week, put it in labeled bags for each day and store them on a long table. They also have a row of hooks in the laundry room with several tote bags with labels like "Pool for Brody" and "Cub Scouts for Cole." All the bags get packed on Sunday for the whole week. Jody and her husband just grab the right bags for the day and head out the door. What a great mom idea!

When both of our kids were in preschool, Dan and I talked about ways to make the mornings less hectic. One idea that really worked was laying out five school outfits for each of our kids on a guest bed every Sunday night. Each day, they chose which outfit to wear, so they had a say in what they wore and we no longer scrambled around at the break of dawn searching for matching socks. I also had a drawer in the kitchen where I kept the things my kids needed when they were doing their homework at the kitchen table—notebook paper, pencils, erasers, tape, glue, rulers—so they knew where to find them *and* where to put them back!

We wanted our kids to value organization and begin learning to do it on their own, so when they were toddlers, we put pictures on the toy bins that indicated what toys went into each bin. We had the Lego bin, the ball bin and the doll bin, and each child had a bookshelf. We had a plastic container with four drawers in the bottom of the closet with one name on each drawer, and that's where we kept mittens, gloves, hats and scarves for each of us. Twice a year we cleaned out the kids' rooms, the playroom and the art area together, giving away clothes that didn't fit, toys they no longer used and art supplies that had dried up. It's definitely easier to be organized when there are fewer things to organize!

One day I got so frustrated with finding colored pencils, markers and crayons *everywhere* that I bought small covered plastic containers for them—another sanity saver. I also kept plastic tablecloths with the school supplies and the art supplies so the kids could use them and not worry about getting marker ink on my table. We also put an old table in the art-supply area that the kids could paint directly on, and I bought a fishing-tackle box with drawers full of art supplies at a charity auction to help us keep our supplies organized.

And it's not just about keeping the kids organized. You need to be organized, too. I'm certain that nearly all of you have had the misfortune of being late to work or school because you couldn't find your car keys. One time I found my keys in the refrigerator, and that was the last straw. I installed key hooks next to the door to hang our keys on the minute we walk in the door. I bought a five-bin laundry hamper so that laundry was pre-sorted by color—whites, red, darks and lights, with an additional bin for dry cleaning—which allowed the kids to sort their own laundry. Every little thing helps when there aren't enough minutes in the day.

Start Small

If just reading this chapter is making you anxious, take a deep breath. You can start small. Pick one thing you continually misplace and give it a home. If you have the same trouble with keys that I did, consider putting a key bowl next to the door or putting up a hook so that whenever you walk in the door, you put your keys on the hook or in the bowl and they stay there until you walk *out* the door. Or pick one problem that makes you crazy—for me it was the markers and crayons, for you it could be shoes—and invest in something to store it in and a permanent place for it to live. Speaking of shoes, I got so fed up with having everyone's shoes scattered all over the house that I put a basket in the family room and any shoes I ran across went into it. Sometimes I even threatened to charge the kids to get them back! I did the same thing for our Wii remotes and gadgets. We even had a basket for the dog's toys.

When my kids were in elementary school, I had to assign a place for birthday-party invitations because I was constantly opening them and immediately losing them. I started getting organized by clipping the invitation to the "sanity bible" immediately after I opened it and writing the date on the calendar. When I bought the gift, I wrapped it and placed it with the invitation on a specific table in our living room. The day of the party, I'd just grab the gift and the invitation and we'd be on our way. (It always helps to have the invitation with you so you know where you're going!)

Jeanne Saunders took this a step further when her two daughters were young. "My middle name is *organized*. I did as much ahead of time as I could. For example, I bought a lot of Barbies one year and wrapped them, knowing I could just whip one out of the closet when needed. The added bonus of being organized is that both of my girls are highly organized and think ahead. Funny how that works!"

The Summer Organization Challenge

Staying organized during the school year and staying organized during the summer may require different skill sets for some of us. For me, summers were an especially difficult time to stay organized because summers lack the same routine as the school year and full-time child care was a challenge. There were so many things we all wanted to do, and the kids needed rides for most of the activities they wanted to participate in. Each year I'd create a folder with information about all the activities they could take part in that provided child care. Then I'd print out a calendar that showed all the possibilities and how they overlapped. The kids and I would look at the calendar together and talk about their priorities. They'd circle the things they really wanted to do and put checkmarks by the activities that were "maybes." And then we'd map out the summer. I hired high school or college kids to fill in around the activities with additional child care.

During the summer, I kept up my practice of making all our meals for the week on Sundays, but with erratic schedules, I discovered that I had to have extra food on hand for quick snacks. There were always healthy things in the refrigerator to heat up, and as a backup I kept "heat and eat" meals and snacks in the freezer so that there were never any panicked trips to the grocery store. Well, almost never!

Being Organized at Work

The three-ring circus of my life definitely spilled over into work after I became a mom. I remember many days when I walked out the door to the airport praying that the shoes in my suitcase matched and that I had the right client files in my briefcase. This was especially challenging when the kids were young and sleep was not in abundance—it's hard to think straight on three hours of sleep. I was constantly waking up in hotels hoping that I was in the right city on the right day.

My desire to find ways to be more organized at work was driven by my desire not only to perform well at work but also to be efficient at work so that I had more time with my kids. I am not a naturally process-oriented person, but I found that doing things the same way every time instead of reinventing the wheel every day made a huge difference when it came to being organized. When the kids were young and I traveled every week while I was at FMI, I kept my plane tickets (yes, they were paper!) in the same place in my briefcase, parked my car in the same area of the airport parking garage and put all my travel receipts in the same briefcase pocket to make doing expense reports easy. When I was president of the Women's Foundation of Colorado, my wonderful executive assistant, Marijke Swierstra, helped me devise a folder system to stay organized. Checks that need to be signed were in a green folder that I knew I needed to tackle every day. My paisley folder had everything in it that I needed to take home and review that evening. The orange folder had all the invitations I received to work-related events so that I could review them all at once and decide which ones to attend. A beige folder had all my mail that wasn't urgent. Of course, this one was regularly ignored until it was too big to carry!

Summary

I'm not the perfectly organized person I'd love to be. Believe me, I still misplace things. The kids were very amused the day I was walking around the house saying, "Where's my cell phone?" and it was in my hand. But a little organization can go a long way toward keeping your family organized and staying sane. Whether you're naturally organized or not, sitting down and coming up with tactics to keep you organized can make a major difference in your life and your kids' lives.

'I'm a Great Working Mom' Exercises

1. What one thing could I organize this week that would simplify my life?

_____

_____

_____

_____

_____

_____

2. Who is the most organized person I know?

_____

_____

3. When can I invite them over to help me organize
   something?

_____

_____

4. What activities cause the most stress in our lives?

_____

_____

_____

_____

_____

_____

_____

_____

_____

5. What can I do to organize these activities? (Do them
   the night before? Have the kids help do them?)

_____

_____

_____

_____

_____

_____

_____

_____

6. How can I improve my weekly and/or monthly schedule?

_____

_____

_____

_____

_____

_____

_____

_____

_____

7. Where do we/should we keep it?

_____

_____

Sanity Savers

- Organize our time and space to free up time and reduce stress.

- Keep a master calendar where all family members can see it.

- Plan further ahead.

- Involve your kids in schedule planning.

- Commit to keeping some open space in your calendars/lives.

- Designate a place for everything in your home and work space.

STEP EIGHT

Give as Much to Yourself as You Give to Others
You're worth it!

I was in a meeting with Megan Ferland, then executive director of the Colorado Children's Campaign, when my heart started skipping beats. Not just periodically but about once every three minutes or so. I'd been having these irregular heartbeats for a few weeks and they were happening more often. Of course, I'd ignored them because I didn't have time to go to the doctor.

I tried to ignore them during the meeting, but I started to feel anxious and that made it worse. Even though I'm not a doctor, I know that a heart should beat in a regular rhythm. Finally, I said to Megan, "I'm really sorry to end our meeting, but I'm having a heartbeat problem and I think I need to go to my doctor. Right now."

And I did. After a few days of testing, I learned that I have premature ventricular and atrial contractions. My doctor put me on a beta-blocker that I'll take for the rest of my life and told me that although the condition isn't life-threatening, it's probably caused by stress and I absolutely had to "cut back" on life.

This was a huge wake-up call for me. I felt fortunate that I'd been given a chance to take better care of myself, and it prompted me to make some major life changes. I resigned from four of the six boards I was serving on.

(Really, who can possibly juggle that many?) I started doing yoga four or five days a week. I made a promise to start doing something fun with a friend every week. I stopped drinking caffeine and bid a fond farewell to the cigars I'd enjoyed smoking while playing golf. The doctors assured me I wouldn't die from this condition, and I believed them but I wasn't about to take any chances. I made a firm commitment to do whatever it took to manage my health. Bottom line: I'm no good to anyone if I'm not here. And the same goes for you!

We must be willing to give ourselves what we need to be healthy, not just physically but in all areas of our lives—the mental, the spiritual, the creative, everything. Women are naturally givers and we do a great job of supporting and nurturing our kids, partners, parents and siblings, but most of us don't do such a great job of nurturing ourselves. If we don't manage the stress of juggling motherhood and work, it can really catch up with us. I'm a perfect example of that.

The Gift of Time

When my kids were growing up, my secret indulgence was playing video games. Really. No one who knows me believes it. Playing video games was a great way to tune out work, and it was fun to keep the kids on their toes by beating them once in a while! They thought it was cool that Mom knew how to play Lego Star Wars—well, until they were teenagers and it wasn't cool anymore. Someone found out my secret because, ten years ago, my son's hockey team gave me a video-gaming chair as my team-manager gift. The looks on the faces of the other players' parents were priceless!

We all have things we'd love to spend more time doing. It doesn't matter what other people may think about our hobbies—what's important is that you value yourself enough to make fun and relaxation a part of your life. You'll be a better mom, partner, sister, daughter, friend and worker if you take time for yourself. Go out with your friends to a movie, read a novel, go for a walk. Get a manicure or a pedicure or both! We all need to relax and have fun, so be sure you're fitting in time every week to do something you enjoy—without feeling guilty about it.

Partner Time

If you're in a relationship, you also need to build in couple's time. No matter how important your kids are to you, your relationship with your partner and the effort to nurture that relationship is just as important. You set an important example for your kids by taking time for each other. At least twice a month, nurture your relationship by going on a date, trying something new together or just kicking back and relaxing without the kids. This doesn't have to cost a lot of money. Some of the best "dates" are walks in the park, a simple picnic, trading massages and other bonding activities that keep your relationship strong and healthy. And remember that our partners need some alone time, too. Encourage them to spend some time having fun with their friends.

Many people don't go out because they don't have someone they trust who can watch their kids. In these days of cell phones and instant communication, I can't believe that everyone doesn't know at least one person who can be trusted with their kids. If this is the reason you're not spending time with your partner away from your kids, reread Step Five, about building a support network. Make a list of nearby family members, adults and teenagers in your neighborhood whom you feel good about and ask your friends and co-workers if they have recommendations for you. Take the time to find someone you trust—they're out there. You need the break, and your kids will benefit from the exposure to someone new.

A lot of working moms don't go out with their partners or their friends because they can't afford to spend the extra money for a baby-sitter. This is another opportunity for you to come up with a creative solution. Maybe you can trade time with another couple who have kids about the same age as yours. Two Saturday nights a month you take their kids, and two Saturday nights a month they take yours. Maybe you can find an elderly neighbor who's lonely and would love to spend time with your kids. Maybe there's something you can do for someone to repay them for baby-sitting, like cutting their hair or doing their nails. Or join a baby-sitting co-op like Jeanne Saunders did. A little ingenuity goes a long way.

Feed Your Sense of Humor

One of the easiest ways to reduce stress and keep life in perspective is to maintain your sense of humor. Laughter is a great stress-reliever. When people annoy you, channel your favorite comedian and find something funny or amusing in the situation. When people on airplanes persisted in asking me who was taking care of my kids, it did annoy me a little at first, but instead of devoting energy to being angry or frustrated by their comments, I chose to maintain my sense of humor and craft a sarcastic retort. I tend to be a serious person at times, and there are days when my kids would have told you I have no sense of humor at all, but I love to laugh and I know it's good medicine, so I go out of my way for comic relief.

My friend Shannon Oury is a big believer in laughter, too, and she's discovered that a good old-fashioned prank can be a great stress-reliever. "Last Halloween, while having drinks with some friends, we hatched a plan to prank our teenagers that had missed their curfew. Four normally reasonable adults hid in the garage with chain saws (no chains) and a hedge trimmer, waiting for our teenagers, and scared the snot out of them! This resulted in much foul language from said teenagers and a broken door when they tried to break it down to get into the house!" Now, that's the way to keep your sense of humor *and* get even with your kids!

Keeping a sense of humor when things don't go as planned is hard but just as important as keeping it when things are going well. If we can find a humorous way to solve a problem, it's a double win.

I'm not certain Dan found this solution to a change in plans humorous, but I sure did. Our kids were in second and third grades and I'd talked Dan into chairing the school's annual giving campaign. Our goal was to get a gift of any amount from every family, so I suggested we stand in the car line at school and collect donations when parents dropped off and picked up their kids. I figured we could introduce ourselves to the parents and ask them to make a small donation so we could reach our 100 percent participation goal.

Then I got the call that I had to leave town that day for a client meeting. I could have flipped out, and my husband could have been furious, which he had a right to be—it was my idea, after all. Instead of being defeated by this sudden change of plans, I set out to find a funny way to deal with it. I blew up a picture of my head to life-size proportions, mounted in on a tongue depressor, and suggested that my husband hold it when he stood in the car line that day. The parents and kids thought it was hilarious, especially those who knew us well, and the annual campaign got more attention than it would have if I'd been there in person. It was definitely a humorous win-win solution. I was a great "fake" working mom!

Self-Care Doesn't Just Happen

Self-care isn't going to happen by accident. You need a plan. Think about what you know you need to do to be a healthier, happier person and therefore a great mom. Find ways to reduce your stress. Try meditation or yoga. Walk, ride a bike, do your nails, take a bath. By taking care of yourself, you're ensuring that you can enjoy your kids and that you have the energy to give them what they need.

As part of my own plan, I started playing golf again when the kids could both drive themselves to hockey practice. It took some creativity, though. I realized I hadn't been playing golf because eighteen holes take a big chunk of time and it was hard for me to find time during the week to organize my friends to play. So I started playing nine holes, early every Saturday and Sunday morning, as a single player signing up to play with three strangers. I enjoyed walking and seeing the mountains and wildlife early in the morning, and I was able to exercise by doing something I love to do. I met a lot of interesting people on the course, and I'd be home by nine thirty in the morning, in plenty of time to make breakfast for the kids. A friend recently told me I have a joy for golf that he's never seen in anyone else, so giving myself the gift of golf is truly taking care of myself. What a great stress-reliever to hit the heck out of that little white ball!

Tips from Other Great Moms

"I take care of myself as much as I can now, but it wasn't always that way," Rachel Contizano says. "I took a class about creating self-care plans, and the instructor taught us to make a plan for our emotional, financial, physical, spiritual and intellectual selves. We made these five plans and included how we were going to carry them out, why they were important to us and what we were going to do. I did that last year, and I was able to keep the physical goals, which were about becoming healthier. The exercise is getting me through the stress, and I've lost weight and become much more aware of my body. I have more confidence, too. I actually did a handstand in yoga the other day, and I've never done a handstand my whole life!"

Lucy worked in rehab and says every day was stressful in one way or another. She has a five-year-old and a two-year-old, and between work and home, her stress was sky-high. "I finally got in touch with what I needed and I got a gym membership," she says. "I go three or four times a week. It's a big stress release, and it gives me more energy for myself and my kids."

Sharon Knight and her friends worked out at the same gym and brought their kids with them. "Working out was really important to me, so I had a group of friends with kids and we'd carve out time we would all go to the gym together," she says. "The kids would go in the pool, the parents would take turns doing fitness routines or swimming and everybody would get what they needed. It took a lot of time, and some of the household stuff didn't get done as well, but for sanity purposes, it was really important to do."

Jeanne Saunders taught her young daughters to give her a few minutes to lie down and rest sometimes when she got home from work and was exhausted. "The baby-sitter would leave and they would immediately be like 'Mommy, Mommy, Mommy.' And I would say, 'Just a minute. I'm going to lie down for twenty minutes, and unless you are bleeding or throwing up, you cannot disturb me.' And I'd go into my room, shut the door, get into bed and fall asleep for about fifteen minutes. When I woke up, I was completely refreshed and able to deal with my girls."

So that they all got some fresh air and exercise, Jeanne started the habit of taking a walk together after dinner. "I needed the exercise and couldn't justify more time away from my girls to go to a health club, so we walked together almost every evening. Whether it was nice weather or it was raining, storming or snowing, we were out there. My girls loved having my complete attention to tell me what happened at school that day, vying for 'air time.' It was wonderful quality time that the three of us had that they still remember fondly."

These women had more great ideas of how to take care of themselves:

"You know, one of the things that I've just always tried to remind myself of is to take care of myself. I think it's probably very common among moms—we can get so wrapped up in trying to take care of everybody else that we neglect ourselves."

—Gloria Bokenkamp

"I did nothing for the first six years, and that was a big mistake. I gained weight and felt bad. Then I started running and kayaking and was much happier. I figured out how to do most of it early in the morning without disrupting the family schedule. As the kids got older, I started taking girls weekends to do more for myself."

—Shannon Oury

"On the weekend when my girls went to their dad's house, I would occasionally stay in bed all day watching movies, just to regroup and recover and be energized for the next week."

—Jeanne Saunders

"I ran, often at four thirty to five thirty in the morning with girlfriends in the same situation. It was the cheapest therapy on the planet."

—Leslie Mitchell

"You have to make time for yourself. Nails, spa, walks, reading—anything that allows you to treat yourself well."

—Margaret Kelly

"Don't give up on treats for yourself, whether it's a manicure, a pedicure, a spa day, or just sitting on your rear end. I don't think anybody should feel guilty about taking care of themselves. One of the things I do is go back home to Omaha a couple of times a year to be with friends. I enjoy having time when I don't have to be a wife and mom!"

—Lisa Walker

"I like to get my nails done. Not only is it relaxing for me, it helps me feel more put together when I'm really not!"

—Deidre Bacala

"I do lots to take care of myself. My favorites are going to the spa, having a massage and meeting friends for lunch."

—Betsy Mordecai

When the kids were little, my Aunt Jo taught me a neat trick for carving out time for myself on Saturday mornings. Starting when the kids were about three and four, I told them that whatever time they woke us up on Saturday morning was the time they would go to bed on Saturday night. If they woke us up at 6:00 am, they went to bed at 6:00 pm. If they woke us up at 7:00 am, they went to bed at 7:00 pm. I put out bowls of cereal the night before and put milk in a small jug in the fridge so that they could fix their own breakfast. They felt "cool" that they could get up, fix breakfast and turn on cartoons, and we got to sleep in. Thank you, Aunt Jo—another great mom!

We all know that it's sometimes hard to carve out time to do what we need to do for ourselves, but I'm convinced that it's the most important thing we can do for our kids and ourselves. I set a goal early in life to earn a degree every year—part of my commitment to focusing on being a life-long learner. It was tough to do my second master's at night school when the kids were young, but it set the example for them that you're never too old to learn, and I was a better mom because I was keeping my commitment to myself. Even significant time commitments like this are important, and your kids will understand your need to carve out time for yourself. Mine did.

How to Make Self-Care Happen

Ever since my wake-up call with my irregular heart rhythm, I've written annual, quarterly and monthly goals for self-care in my journal. I have a recurring appointment for golf in my Google calendar every Saturday and Sunday morning and a recurring appointment to "work out"—yoga or Zumba or both—every day. Each week I decide what four days I *really* can work out and adjust my calendar if necessary.

When we're busy, we can't count on spontaneously being able to see our friends. So, a few years ago I set a goal to do one fun thing every week with friends, and I enter these into my calendar as well. We go to a movie, go out to dinner or, if I'm really crunched, just have a quick drink. I work hard to make this happen every week, and my kids understand how important this time is to me.

Remember, it's not just about taking physical care of ourselves. Emotional care is important, and at times I've sought help with this by seeing a psychologist. Just as we visit a doctor if we don't feel physically well, I think it's important to seek out psychological help when we don't feel mentally well. "Unwellness" comes in many forms—anxiety, depression, a lack of self-worth. It's important to realize when you aren't at your mental best and seek help. It's not a sign of weakness, it's a sign of strength.

The same is true of asking for any kind of help when we need it. "It's hard to ask for help, but it's really important that we're strong enough to do it when we need it," says Gail, a single working mom. "And I've learned that it takes strength to accept help, even when we don't ask for it."

"One way we can take care of ourselves is to accept where we are and focus on where we're going," says Ruby. "For the longest time, I couldn't get over the fact that I was a single mom and had to apply for food stamps to feed my daughter. That was a waste of energy. Don't be ashamed of your situation. Just work on making things better."

Financial care is important as well. I switched to a new financial advisor after my divorce. Steph is my partner in planning my future—how I'll pay for college for my kids and all the goals that are important to me. She's a great source of support and encouraged me to take three months off from work to be with my elderly mom before her death, one of the best decisions I ever made. Steph knew that I had the resources to do it and that if I didn't do it, I'd regret it for the rest of my life. I was so thankful to be able to spend more time with my mom during her last year, to be there when she told me, "I love you," the day before she passed away.

Summary

On the plane, they say, "Put *your* own oxygen mask on first." That's what we all need to do. We aren't great moms if we don't take care of ourselves. We're no good to employers and no good to family if we aren't taking care of ourselves. So please take care of yourself. Be kind to yourself. Be as kind to yourself as you are to everyone around you. You're a great mom and you deserve it.

'I'm a Great Working Mom' Exercises

1. I commit to doing the following for myself:

   _____

   _____

   _____

   _____

   _____

   _____

   _____

   _____

   I will do it _____ times a year/month.

2. My partner commits to doing the following for him/ herself:

   _____

   _____

   _____

   _____

   _____

   _____

   _____

   He/she will do it _____ times a year/month.

3. My partner and I commit to going out on a date _____ times a month.

4. People I trust to watch my kids:

_____

_____

_____

_____

_____

_____

_____

_____

Sanity Savers

- Make a firm commitment to do whatever it takes to manage your health.

- Be willing to give yourself what you need to be healthy, not just physically but in all areas of life.

- Value yourself enough to make fun and relaxation part of your daily life!

- Nurture your relationship with your partner.

- Keep life in perspective and avoid taking yourself—and your kids—too seriously.

- Laugh more. Stress less.

CLOSING NOTE

I can still hear the sound of my twenty-two-month-old daughter sobbing as I walked in the door. I'd stopped to get a much-needed haircut after work. My husband, Dan, who was holding Regan, said something like "There's been an accident." I was immediately panicked and, of course, chastised myself for not having been there. Sound familiar? The internal voice of guilt.

It turns out Regan and her three-year-old brother had been playing with their cousins in Holden's bedroom. As Regan climbed up the bunk-bed ladder to join the boys, her brother thought better of that and gave her a nudge (that's the polite version of this story). Dan heard a thud, followed by Regan's wailing.

I checked Regan over from head to toe and didn't find any signs of injury, but I couldn't shake the feeling that something was wrong. I called my brother-in-law, a doctor, and he suggested I give her Tylenol and said that if she could sleep, she was probably OK. Regan slept through the night, but I couldn't shake the nagging feeling that something was wrong with her arm. I was supposed to take the day off and go skiing with Dan and his family, but I told him, "I really feel like I should take Regan to the doctor." Dan poked a little fun at me but drove off to ski while I called the doctor.

When we arrived at the doctor's office, Regan's pediatrician, a woman, felt her arm and didn't think anything was wrong, but trusted my "mom's intuition" and sent us off to Children's Hospital Colorado for an X-ray. I hadn't thought to pack lunch, so we made do with Lunchables from a convenience store on the way.

The X-ray confirmed my instincts. Regan had buckle-fractured two bones in her arm just above her wrist. I was devastated. I forced myself to keep it together as we went to the office of an orthopedic doctor, where Regan picked out a purple cast for her arm. She didn't cry once the whole day even though she never had a nap and didn't have much to eat.

When we finally got back home that afternoon, I burst into tears. How could I have let this happen to my daughter? I didn't feel like a great mom—I felt like a horrible mom. Dan called from the slope and joked, "Is her arm broken?" Of course, he was shocked when I told him Regan had a purple cast on her arm.

The point is that no matter how much we prepare, how careful we are, how much we love our kids, stuff happens. We are not *perfect* moms. We are great moms. All of us are doing our best, every day, and things will still happen. Please get over the guilt. We are not torturing our kids, starving them, beating them. We are loving them and caring for them, and accidents will happen. Bad parenting moments will happen. My friend Emily Sinclair once told me the story of standing at the back door hollering at her kids and then realizing that a neighbor was watching her over the fence. "It sucks when you're caught in a bad parenting moment!" she said. Emily has a wonderful sense of humor.

Of course, there's no better proof that you're a great mom than hearing it from your grown kids. When I was working on this book, my editor asked if she could interview Holden and Regan to hear what they had to say about growing up with a working mom. I was worried that the label "great mom" might be in danger!

Here's what they had to say:

"The fact that my mom excels in math and became an engineer, even though there were people telling her that she couldn't, and then the way she dealt with sexism in the workplace and rose to the level that she did, and then decided that she wanted to do something completely different and did it, is amazing to me," Holden says. "I'm just really proud of her."

He added: "The kids with the helicopter moms who were always helping them with homework or projects or doing them for them didn't learn how to be independent. I learned to do the work myself, and I also learned a lot about communication, I think. Just talking with mom over the phone if I needed help with math helped me to voice my problem in a way that she could see and understand what I was asking."

Regan said: "Having a mom who worked outside the home definitely taught me to be independent. But I think it also taught me about having balance in life. Not everything's about work or family—you have to find that balance between the two, and I think my mom really did that. She showed us that you can work and have a family and do fun stuff.

"I wasn't envious of my friends whose moms stayed home, but I did sometimes wish my own mom could be home more often. But now I feel like if she had been home, our relationship might not be as great as it is. The relationships most of my friends have with their moms are really different from what my mom and I have, and I definitely think that our relationship is one of the better ones. I wouldn't trade it for anything."

I'm grateful for my kids' kind words. They know I'm not perfect, but they know I've tried my best. More important than anything to me—aside from keeping my kids alive and well—was to develop loving, open relationships with them. Now that they're adults, we still enjoy each other and value spending time together.

"In the midst of all the responsibility and work, remember that in the end it's about developing a loving and mutual relationship with your children," Shannon Oury says. "It will help them with all the other relationships that they will have in life."

The next time you're comparing yourself with stay-at-home moms, maybe Holden's and Regan's comments will help you to think differently. Yes, I know how hard it is to stop yourself. Stay-at-home moms can usually volunteer more at school, chaperone field trips and pick their kids up from school or meet them at the bus stop. They're physically there for their kids most of the time, and they don't have to miss their kids' first steps, new words and daily discoveries. But that doesn't make them better moms, and it doesn't mean they love their kids more than we love ours. I will support both Regan and Holden whether they decide to work outside the home or stay home with their kids. Both decisions are the "right" decision—one will just be better for them.

I hope this book has been helpful for you. I encourage you to pick *one* thing that you think will help you. When you have that mastered, pick *one* more thing to do. Don't try to do it all at once—that will create more stress! Which one of these steps is most important to you right now?

Step 1 – Get over the guilt and feel good about working.

Step 2 – Set realistic expectations for yourself as a mom and an employee.

Step 3 – Don't be afraid to ask for an adjustment of your work schedule.

Step 4 – Create a child-rearing partnership with your partner or someone else.

Step 5 – Build a strong support network of family and friends to help you.

Step 6 – Find the right child care for you so you know the kids are in good hands.

Step 7 – Get organized, get organized, get organized!

Step 8 – Take as much care of yourself as you take of everyone else in your life.

I reread Steven Covey's *Seven Habits of Highly Effective People* every year or two because it helps me stay focused on my personal mission, my roles and my goals in life. In a similar vein, rereading this book periodically will help you make adjustments to the game plan as your life journey continues and your kids get older. Your needs and challenges will morph over time. Things will happen to change the plan. My divorce in 2011 had a significant impact on my game plan, as did my mom's health challenge and eventual death in 2013. Have a plan, but realize that it will need to be adjusted over time. It's like having a playbook in football—the team always makes halftime adjustments.

This book is also just the start of my journey to help working moms feel better about themselves by sharing tips on reducing stress and conquering the juggling act. I encourage you to visit our website, *www.greatworkingmoms.com*, join our LinkedIn Group, Great Working Moms; like us on Facebook at Great Working Moms, and follow us on twitter *@greatworkingmom*. You can also reach me at *gretchen@greatworkingmoms.com*.

And most of all, don't be so hard on yourself. You're doing a good job. Your kids appreciate you. Your employer appreciates you. You need to appreciate you, today and every day.

Remember, you're a great working mom.

A portion of the proceeds from this book will benefit Warren Village, an outstanding Denver nonprofit that has transformed the lives of 4,400 low income families, primarily headed by single women, over the last four decades. Its nationally recognized programs create pathways to economic self-sufficiency by providing affordable housing, on-site accredited child care and education, supportive family services, educational guidance and career development. Several residents provided valuable input for this book. To learn more, please visit *www.warrenvillage.com*.

I am also grateful to my publisher Brent Darnell, Founder of BDI Publishers, for contributing one-third of their profits from this book to Safehouse Outreach's Family & Women Services of Atlanta, Georgia. Safehouse Outreach has been giving the disenfranchised in Atlanta a hand-up, not a hand-out, for more than 25 years. They help women by offering parenting and job skills classes so that they can care for themselves and their children. For more information, please visit *www.safehouseoutreach.org*.